Confident Children

By the same author

ASSERT YOURSELF
MANAGING ANGER
THE POSITIVE WOMAN
SELF ESTEEM
SELF MOTIVATION
SUPER CONFIDENCE

Confident Children

A Parents' Guide to Helping Children Feel Good About Themselves

Gael Lindenfield

Thorsons
An Imprint of HarperCollinsPublishers

Thorsons
An Imprint of HarperCollins*Publishers*
77–85 Fulham Palace Road,
Hammersmith, London W6 8JB
1160 Battery Street,
San Francisco, California 94111–1213

Published by Thorsons 1994
5 7 9 10 8 6 4

A catalogue record for this book
is available from the British Library

ISBN 0 7225 2824 8

Printed in Great Britain by
Caledonian International Book Manufacturing Ltd, Glasgow

To Laura, my daughter who takes her first
strides into the adult world this year – with
deepest love, constant admiration and unending
gratitude for enriching my life and teaching
me so much about parenting.

Acknowledgements

Although I am acknowledged as the author of this book, I know that many of the ideas and strategies it contains have been born as a result of wisdom which I have acquired from hundreds and hundreds of other people. In particular, I would like to thank:

- All the participants on my courses who have shared so honestly about their childhoods and their own struggles with confidence and parenting, and then courageously experimented with new approaches and strategies.
- My two daughters, Susie and Laura and my step-daughter, Sarah who have all helped me learn so much from both my parenting mistakes and my successes.
- Jessica Stockham, who once again has done such creative and humourous illustrations.

And finally,

- Stuart my husband, for his constant emotional support and his willingness to drop, on demand, all his other many roles in life to become my personal 'in-house' editor.

Contents

List of Exercises

Introduction

Have you ever found yourself feeling jealous of a pheasant? I did, just a few months ago. I was visiting our local zoo, Marwell, which specializes in breeding and taking care of endangered species, and I came across a beautiful rare pheasant. When I read the note on her cage, I felt a surge of envy. It seems that this lucky bird was currently being given a chance to 'practise her parenting skills' by temporarily caring for a number of surrogate chicks. I turned to my husband and said, 'It's not fair – all my practice had to take place on Susie and Laura!'

This book is an attempt to provide a more considered, adult response to my concerns about the dangers of 'not good-enough' parenting. For many years I have been surrounded by evidence that has convinced me that, in this fast-changing, complex, competitive jungle of a world there is another endangered species – the confident parent! I wonder if you have even met one: I am talking about a relaxed, guilt-free creature who seems *naturally* and *effortlessly* to be able to produce a complete breed of equally happy, confident and competent children. Like me, you are probably much more familiar with the kind of parents who spend a considerable amount of time worrying about whether they are 'getting it right', or feeling guilty because they know that they are often 'getting it wrong'!

Is the problem that we now know too much? Should we simply

burn those child psychology books and parenting magazines which have raised our expectations of good-enough parenting to seemingly impossible heights?

I don't think so, because even though the image of the carefree cave-parent is sometimes very tempting, I cannot believe that either children or parents would have much to gain from turning the clock back. As you have chosen to read this book, I am assuming that you also believe that we now have a responsibility to use the knowledge and wisdom our culture has given us to develop and improve the emotional well-being of our children.

The suggestions and strategies in this book are offered as constructive alternatives to the paralysing anxiety and self-reproach which often seems to attack us when, in spite of our loving efforts, our children behave in a way which could indicate that their confidence is at a low ebb. For example, if we find that they are showing signs of:

- clinging on too long to 'babyish habits' such as thumb-sucking or bed-wetting
- under-achieving at school because they are too timid to ask for help or they feel lonely
- getting over-concerned with their work and requiring it to be too perfect
- becoming reluctant to venture from the safety of their home or town
- being frustratingly unable to make up their mind or give an opinion
- becoming immobilized with anxiety, fears, phobias or obsessions
- waking each night with frightening nightmares
- behaving shyly or inappropriately at social occasions
- becoming over-sensitive to criticism or teasing
- developing physical symptoms of stress such as headaches, nausea, or skin rashes
- showing off or bullying
- becoming persistently jealous or envious of others
- rejecting compliments and giving themselves put-downs
- losing their appetite or compulsively bingeing

In spite of being super-conscious of the vast numbers of parents who are crying out for help and guidance to help them tackle (or, indeed, prevent) such common problems. I had some initial misgivings about writing this book. First, you may be comforted to know that I was all too aware of my own mistakes as a mother. Secondly, I was working against a deeply held sense of mistrust in parenting 'bibles', which I believed could inhibit parents from using their natural nurturing intuition. After some reflection, I came to the conclusion that in an ideal world pheasants would not need parenting practise and humans might not need books such as this, but in the mean time there was very little excuse for not sharing my own personal and professional insights.

Who is this book for?

I have written this self-help programme for any thoughtful parents who are keen to do some constructive, ongoing practical personal development work which will enable them to become more effective in their efforts to build their children's confidence. Although it contains many tips and guidelines, it has never been my intention that any of the material in this book should be used by robots looking for categorical operating instructions!

I anticipate that this book may also make interesting reading for many people who are *in loco parentis* (such as partners of parents, grandparents, child-minders, teachers and youth workers); it could also be used as a resource for professionals who are engaged in teaching parenting skills.

Finally, much of the material in the last half of this book (e.g. guidelines on successful communication and assertiveness) may also be of direct interest to older children.

What this book offers

- An explanation of the nature of confidence and how its particular components and strengths can help children become not only happier, but more able to make full use of their personal potential

- An insight into the kind of qualities in parents, their families and their homes which have been found to affect the development of children's confidence
- Guidelines on what actions parents can take and what language they should use, if they wish to build or boost their children's confidence
- Instructions on how to teach children useful social skills such as communication, assertiveness and the management of their feelings
- Simple strategies to use (and teach children to use) for dealing with problems and conflicts in a positive manner
- Tips on how to help children make transitions from home to the outside world successfully
- A programme of exercises which can be used by parents (working on their own or in small groups) to reinforce what they have learned from this book and to encourage them to translate its suggestions into appropriate action

How to use this book

As I have already indicated, this book is designed as an ongoing self-help programme. You will probably gain most benefit from first reading it through relatively quickly and then returning to it for a second reading at a slower pace, giving yourself time to do the exercises and to try out the guidelines and suggestions.

If you are 'in partnership' with a co-parent, ideally it would be best if you were to work even more slowly through the book together. Rarely do two people ever fully agree on parenting issues and, to some degree, this is a fact of life (albeit an uncomfortable one) which both children and parents must learn to accept and respect. But working jointly on this programme will at least give you a chance to discuss, argue and, hopefully, agree on some basic *joint* strategies and approaches.

Because this book has been written quite generally for parents with children of varying ages and abilities, you may sometimes need to 'translate' the text and adapt the exercises to suit your specific needs, your particular children and the culture in which you are living.

Finally, I hope that once you have completed the programme you will find this book a useful and supportive reference to refer to from time to time while your children are growing up. Please remember that it should be seen first and foremost as *your* resource, to be adapted and modified to suit your needs. I know from my own experience that reading books like this often stimulates my thinking and creativity, so if you come up with any new ideas as you read, please keep me informed!

Part 1
Personal development work for parents

Chapter 1
Understanding more about confidence

In recent years the word 'confidence' seems to have acquired a fashionable 'buzz'. Cars, computers, insurance policies, football players and even lipsticks are being sold on the basis that they are 'confident' performers. The word itself has acquired a variety of meanings for different people. Our first task, therefore, must be to clarify exactly what we mean when we use the word confidence in relation to people.

A very wide definition with which most people may agree might be: 'Confident people are people who feel OK about themselves.'

For general communication purposes, this rather vague concept is quite adequate, but we soon realize its limitations when we start trying to summon up more of this important 'OK' stuff for either ourselves or our children. It is at this point that we realize how vital it is to have a clearer idea of what exactly we are searching for.

When I was asked to write my book *Super Confidence*, I was fortunately forced to do some long, hard thinking around the definition of confidence and come up with an analysis of its specific components. I did this by listing the qualities and skills I had observed in people with a high degree of self-confidence. I have since found that this list has proved extremely useful in a number of ways. First, it has enabled me to plan and lead much more effective confidence-building programmes. Secondly, it has helped participants on my courses, and my readers, not to feel so overwhelmed by their 'lack of confidence' because their problem had been broken down into more manageable 'bite-sized chunks'. Thirdly, it has proved to be an invaluable checklist. For example, when I find my own confidence ebbing (and of course it does from time to time), I can go through the list and quickly identify where the 'weak spots' are and then put into action a rescue plan for my own mental health!

When I started to do my 'confidence analysis', it soon became clear that there were in fact two fairly distinct types: *inner* and *outer*. The inner kind is the one that gives us the *feeling* and *belief* that we are OK; the outer kind enables us to *appear* and *behave* in a manner which denotes to the outside world that we are self-assured. And, because the inner and outer kinds of confidence support each other, together they make for something much more powerful and effective than the sum of their parts.

Let's now examine both kinds of confidence in more depth and see what bearing the components of each might have on the feelings, behaviour and performance of our children. As you read the next two sections, mark or note down the particular components that are of interest to you. Perhaps these might be ones which you feel need boosting or developing in your own child or children, or they may be ones which your own life experience has taught you are especially important.

Inner confidence

There are four main hallmarks which identify people who have a sound sense of inner confidence. These are:

- self-love
- self-knowledge
- clear goals
- positive thinking

Self-love

Confident people love themselves and, moreover, their self-love is not a well-hidden secret. It is obvious to the outsider that they care about themselves because their behaviour and lifestyle are self-nurturing. With this component of inner confidence children will, for example:

- retain their natural inclination to value both their physical and emotional needs and place these on an *equal* footing with the needs of others
- feel quite justified in their attempts to get these needs met; they will not inwardly torture themselves with guilt every time they ask for, or get, something they want
- be open in their demands for praise, reassurance and rewards and not try to manipulate you or anyone else into giving these indirectly
- enjoy being nurtured by others and become experts at learning how to do this for themselves
- feel proud of their good features and concentrate on making the most of these; they will not want to waste too much time, energy or money on their own imperfections
- want to be healthy and so will (eventually!) take heed of the wisdom about brushing their teeth, eating sensibly and keeping fit
- not knowingly persist in doing things that will sabotage their chances of success and happiness or shorten their lives

Self-knowledge

Inwardly confident people are also very self-aware. They do not stare constantly at their own navels, but they do regularly reflect on their feelings, thoughts and behaviour and are always interested to know how they are being perceived by others. If children develop good self-knowledge they will, for example:

- be very aware of their strengths and therefore be much more able to meet their full potential

- know their weaknesses and limitations and therefore be less likely to set themselves up constantly for failure
- grow up with a firm sense of their own identity and therefore be much more able and content to become an 'individual' and not sheepishly follow 'the crowd'
- have a sound sense of their own values so they will not be constantly fretting about whether or not the things they or others are doing (or not doing) are morally justified
- are more likely to have friends who are 'right' for them because they know what qualities they need from friendship
- be open to taking feedback from others and not always leaping on the defensive at the first hint of criticism
- be willing and eager to take constructive help and tuition because they are not 'know-alls'

Clear goals

There is almost always a sense of purpose surrounding confident people. This is because they have a clear idea of why they are taking a particular course of action and of the kind of results they can realistically expect. With this ingredient bolstering up their inner confidence children will, for example:

- get in the habit of *setting themselves* achievable goals; they will not always need to be dependent on others to 'make' them do things
- have more energy and excitement because they will be motivated
- have more persistence because they will see even the small and sometimes boring steps forward as having a purpose
- learn the important art of self-evaluation because they will be able to monitor their progress in the light of the goals they have set themselves
- find decision-making relatively easy because they have a clear idea of what they want and need from the outcome

Positive thinking

Confident people are usually great company; one of the reasons why is that they are in the habit of seeing the brighter side of life and will be expecting and looking for good experiences and outcomes. With this important inner strength children will, for example:

- grow up expecting life to be generally good
- think the best of people unless there is a particular reason to be wary
- believe that most problems have a solution
- not waste energy worrying about *possible* negative outcomes
- believe that the future has the potential to be as good (if not better) than the past
- be willing to work through the uncomfortable frustrations of change because they like the excitement of growth and development
- be prepared to put time and energy into learning – and doing the necessary 'ground work' – because they believe that their goals will eventually be achieved.

Outer confidence

In order to convey a confident impression to the rest of the world, your child will also need to develop skills in the following four areas:

- communication
- assertiveness
- self-presentation
- emotional control

It's no wonder that the priciest private schools and the very best state schools put so much emphasis on the attainment of these skills as well as academic achievements, because they know that children who have these will not only have a headstart in the

SOME RELEVANT STAGES IN CHILD DEVELOPMENT

1–2½ years
starting to use language; developing a sense of self

2½–5 years
trying to gain some control over environment and own care; testing out new memory and comprehension skills; experimenting with own feelings

5–11 years
wanting to learn, achieve, create and be active; starting to make friends and explore outside world; testing out own and others' aggression; exploring own sexuality and experimenting with gender roles

Adolescence
wanting to be accepted by peer group; searching and experimenting with own identity; challenging rules and developing moral judgement; looking for a sense of purpose in life; wanting to gain control over bodily imperfections; testing ability to love and be loved through passionate relationships; experimenting with independence from parents; testing own skills and physical and intellectual strengths

adult world of work but will also stand a better chance of having a fulfilling personal and social life.

Let's consider, in turn, how each of these could benefit your children.

Communication

With a good grounding in communication skills children will, for example, be able to:

- listen accurately, calmly and empathically to other people
- make 'small talk' with people of all ages and all kinds of backgrounds
- know when and how to move conversations on from small talk to a 'deeper' level
- use non-verbal communication effectively so that this matches their verbal language
- read, and make use of, the body language of others
- discuss and argue both rationally and articulately
- speak in public without being paralysed with anxiety

Assertiveness

If we teach our children to be assertive, they will rarely have to resort to aggressive and passive tactics in order to get what they want out of life and relationships. Their confidence will be enhanced because they will, for example, be able to:

- express their needs directly and straightforwardly
- stand up for their rights and those of others
- know how to negotiate acceptable compromises
- give and receive compliments freely and sensitively
- give and receive constructive criticism
- complain and campaign effectively

Self-presentation

This skill will teach children the importance of 'looking the part' of a confident person. It will enable them to:

- choose overall dress styles and colours that make the most of their *individual* personality and physical attributes
- choose clothes that are appropriate for different roles and occasions while still maintaining their own personal style
- gain credibility fast by making good 'first impressions'
- be aware of the impact of lifestyle symbols (e.g. car, house, etc.) on other people's perception of them without being restricted by a desire to please others continually

Emotional control

If feelings are not managed well, they can wield enormous unpredictable power. Sometimes it is good fun and exciting to allow our hearts to rule our heads, but generally in the everyday course of our lives we need to exercise skills that keep 'the upper-hand' on our emotions. If children have been taught how to keep this kind of control, they will, for example, be able to:

- trust themselves better because they will not be worried that they will act unpredictably

- take on more challenges and risks because they can manage their fear, anxiety and frustration
- grieve healthily because they will not be afraid that their sadness will envelop and depress them forever
- cope effectively with confrontation and defend themselves from abuse, because they can use the energy of their anger in constructive ways
- allow themselves to be spontaneous and 'let their hair down' on occasions when they want to relax, because they do not fear that they may 'go over the top'
- waste energy torturing themselves with guilt when they experience quite natural negative emotions such as jealousy and irritation (instead they will find constructive ways of containing and controlling these feelings)
- seek out experiences and relationships which give them deep joy, love and happiness, because they do not feel overwhelmed by passion

Super confidence

This is the term I use to describe the kind of confidence which is constructed from *all* the above components and, as I said earlier, has some indefinable 'extra' quality. The additional strength and power of Super Confidence derives from the continual supportive interaction between its inner and outer parts.

This is the kind of confidence which the idealist in me would love all children to have developed before they leave the protection of the nest. The realist in me knows, however, that the goal for most parents must be to give their children a 'good-enough' measure of both inner and outer confidence – plus, very importantly, the belief that they themselves can build on these foundations and eventually acquire the 'super' version for themselves in their adult life.

When as parents we are trying to lay down the foundations of confidence for our children, I think it is important to remember that we need to achieve a good balance between the inner and outer elements. Very often certain parts get developed at the expense of others. Unfortunately, in many ambitious families and schools, for example, too much emphasis may be put on the outer confidence skills. I recently read with interest that Joe Kennedy, the father of the late American president John Kennedy, would say to his children: 'It's not what you are that counts, it's what people think you are.' Perhaps this kind of philosophy was in part responsible for his sons' problems in finding personal peace, in spite of their considerable skills in the area of outer confidence. I have met very many outwardly successful people who have also learned to behave in such a cool, controlled manner that you would find it hard to believe that they are secretly wasting a lot of precious time and energy worrying about whether they will be liked or loved, whether they will be able to 'do it' or 'say it', wondering whether they have made 'the perfect decision' or kicking themselves for having hurt the feelings of an aggressive bully.

In contrast, there are also children who may be full of inner confidence but fail to communicate their strengths to the rest of the world. Others may never know how clear and strong the beliefs and ideas of such people actually are, because they are rarely proffered, and these people may never be given the 'plum opportunities' which they know they deserve, simply because their presence is hardly noticed. And, because they have never learned how to make the best use of their inner confidence, they continually under-achieve and may subsequently become bored, disheartened and depressed.

How is confidence acquired and lost?

Nature or nurture?
Are some of us born lucky? Do some children arrive in the world with a genetic predisposition towards being confident? Many people still believe that they do. They talk about children being

'born shy' or 'born leaders'. To some extent, they are right. We all arrive in the world with a predisposition to develop certain personality traits which are often divided broadly into the categories of behaviour styles – extrovert and introvert – and one could argue that, in our modern competitive culture, the more outgoing children are the more likely they are to thrive both socially and intellectually. But no doubt you have met, as indeed I have, very many 'quietly confident' people who are exceptions to this rule. So, although an inheritance of 'extrovert' genes may be an asset for some children, it certainly brings no guarantee of sound self-confidence. In fact, I am convinced that each one of us arrives in the world with a more or less similar 'starter-package' of basic confidence ingredients, and that we all have the personal potential to build on these foundations. In the first few weeks of life every baby I have had contact with has appeared to have good self-esteem, a positive outlook and the will (if not very sophisticated skills) to ask for what he or she wants. I only wish I could say the same of every five year old child I have met.

Such basic observations (plus of course a few years' acquisition of more sophisticated wisdom!) have left me totally convinced that, with regard to confidence: **it is not so much who we are when we are born that counts, but who we are encouraged and allowed to become.**

So, the basic assumption underlying this book is that it is how we are nurtured rather than our inherited nature that is important to the development of confidence. And it is the quality of that nurturing which determines our ability to hold on to the precious sense of self-esteem we had at birth and build on our potential to become Super Confident adults.

Nowadays the 'nurturing' process of children is a very lengthy and complicated process, and certainly parents do not have the sole responsibility for its progress. Children are 'brought up' and critically influenced not just by mothers and fathers but a seemingly endless list of other people such as childminders, teachers, youth leaders, sports coaches, step-parents – not to mention TV presenters, rock stars and advertising executives! However, in most children's lives I believe that it is still Mum and Dad (natural or otherwise) who wield the most fundamental guiding power. I certainly have yet to meet anyone lacking in self-confidence whose problems cannot be traced back in *some* degree to 'deficient' parenting. No doubt in taking this line I am preaching to the converted, because dedicated opponents of this theory would hardly be motivated to read this book!

So let's move on from the well-worn path of the nature/nurture debate and just reflect on exactly what 'nutrients' children need to receive in the course of their development, if their potential for self-confidence is to be exploited in full. I have found that these can be divided up into the eight main areas summarized below.

1. **Love** – and it's not just quantity but excellent quality that is important. Children need to be loved consistently and *unconditionally*. For the development of sound, lasting self-esteem, they must feel that they are valued for who they actually are, rather than what they could be or what others would like them to be.
2. **Security** – fear and anxiety are perhaps the greatest enemies of confidence. Children who are constantly worried that their basic needs won't be met, or that their emotional or physical world may be blown apart at any minute, will find it very difficult to develop a positive outlook about themselves, other people and the world in general. When children feel secure, they will automatically try to develop their potential (and therefore their confidence) through responding to challenges and taking interesting risks.
3. **Role-models** – teaching through example is by far the most effective way to help children develop the attitudes and social skills required for confidence. People often ask me if they are likely to pass on their fears and anxieties to their children. Of course the depressing answer is – yes, unless a strong countering influence from other significant figures is consistently experienced.
4. **Relationships** – to develop the confidence to relate to 'all sorts', children obviously need to experience and experiment in a wide range of relationships, from the close

20

intimate ones usually found at home through to the more superficial ones with the butcher, the baker and the candlestick maker! Through relationships, children also build up self-awareness and self-knowledge, which are vital ingredients of inner confidence.

5. **Health** – in order to make the best use of our strengths and talents we need energy! We know for example, that children, who are undernourished cannot learn as effectively and are therefore unable to use their full potential. We also know that children 'bloom' when they are in good health – and in our society there is no doubt that good-looking children are likely to receive more morale-boosting compliments, attention and even opportunities.

6. **Resources** – perhaps the children of our ancestors in caves did not need money or material or educational resources in order to help them develop confidence, but we now live in an increasingly complex world. Wrong though it may be, children who have plenty of access to resources such as books, toys, musical instruments, sports facilities, extra tuition and travel certainly have an advantage over those whose options are more restricted. Such resources are not, of course, essential to the development of a core of either inner or outer confidence, but (used well and appropriately) they can certainly give both a powerful boost by providing the kind of opportunities that encourage the development of children's potential by enabling them to use their strengths or improve their weaknesses.

7. **Support** – of course it is not enough to have resources alone, children need encouragement and guidance on how to use them to their best advantage. They need people who are 'rooting' for them to become more confident and skilful, people who will give them honest, constructive feedback both when they are doing well and when they are failing (perhaps through setting themselves unrealistic goals). Support also is an essential factor in helping children heal from the knocks to confidence that trauma,

hurt and disappointment undoubtedly can bring. For example, a rejection by a friend or a failed exam has the capacity to dent self-confidence – but for how long and how deep will depend very much on the kind of support that surrounds a child. I am convinced that it is the 'handling' of traumas and losses rather than the events themselves which plays a decisive role.

8. **Rewards** – although the process of developing confidence (like any other kind of learning) *can* in itself be exciting and rewarding, sometimes it most certainly is not. 'Pay-offs' for efforts and achievements while on the road to our more distant goals are often not just desirable but essential, even for the most ambitious among us. Children are certainly no exception to this pragmatic rule. The ones who are fortunate enough to receive regular and ample 'fruits' (and, of course, I don't mean necessarily material benefits) for their efforts, are far more likely to retain their natural appetites for morale-boosting challenge than those who do not.

Seeing these factors listed in such a concise manner makes the nurturing task look so straightforward and easy! Perhaps it is for a small minority of Super Confident parents who themselves learned the 'trade secrets' from their perfect parents. But I know that my own experience of trying to provide my children with an adequate supply of the above has been the most challenging and difficult undertaking of my life. Even though my heart was certainly in the right place and, because of my professional training, my head was packed full of the right information, my actual ability to provide my children with a consistent supply of these nurturing factors remained woefully deficient for many years.

The good news is that, however *difficult* it is to become the kind of parents who are capable of producing confident, self-assured children, nowadays it is rarely *impossible* for any of us. Present day, post-Freud parents do now have a distinct advantage over those of earlier centuries. We have the tried and tested wisdom of several generations of psychologists, psychotherapists and educationalists to guide us through our parenting. But before we begin to apply this enlightened knowledge directly to our children, we must first make use of it ourselves!

'To respond to our children's needs we must change ourselves. Only when we are willing to undergo the suffering of such changing can we become the kind of parents our children need us to be.'

M. Scott Peck

Chapter 2
How to become a good-enough parent

This chapter was difficult for me to write and may well prove to be the hardest one for you to read and 'take on board'. After all, who likes to be reminded or to be made aware of their shortcomings, especially in relation to their 'sacred' role as parents?! So, as you read you may need to be on your guard for defensive reactions such as denial ('Thank goodness *I'm* not like that') or intellectualizations ('That's a very interesting point but I'm not sure that's quite the right word to use . . .') – or, of course, paralysing guilt reactions. You may find it hard to resist self-flagellation as you are reminded of your sometimes less than perfect parenting. You will just have to make a conscious effort to divert your energies into more constructive channels by planning how you can continue to build on your strengths and overcome your weaknesses. You can start by completing the practical exercises included in this chapter!

Let's start by examining some extremes – the saints and the sinners of the parenting world. We will look first at the positive end of the continuum. I doubt if any such paragons of perfection are actually reading this book – their children already possess superlative self-assurance and outstanding social skills! Nevertheless I am sure the vast majority of you will be able to identify some of your parenting strengths as you read the following list.

The seven 'saintly' characteristics of perfect parents

1. **Strength** – Being sturdy enough to withstand having several people dependent on them for up to two decades; giving their own physical and mental health high priority in their lives so that their children perceive them as robust and reliable and not in need of their support before they are mature enough reasonably to be able to give it. Such parents therefore have the emotional strength to give an endless abundance of 'no-strings-attached' love and a full potential of physical energy to meet the taxing demands of their parenting role.

2. **Sensitivity** – Having the ability to 'fine-tune' into the needs and feelings of others who have not yet developed the capacity to express these adequately themselves. These parents are able to use their intuition to make judgements and decisions to suit each individual child and situation and not rely overly on rules, theories or child-rearing 'bibles'. They are also sensitive to their own feelings and needs and do not live behind emotional screens themselves so that they are open to developing genuinely warm, intimate relationships with people whom they are close to.

3. **Sociability** – Having a lively interest in people and enjoying participation in social events (even though they may prefer these to be small and informal in nature). They value friendships and put time and energy into developing and maintaining these. They are generally recognized as being approachable and friendly and the kind of people who are pleasant and easy to be with at work or in the community in which they live. They ensure that there is always enough space in their lives for fun and lighthearted interactions. Generally, they trust other people and can derive much pleasure and satisfaction from working in partnerships

and teams. They are keen to find opportunities for their children to mix with people from all walks of life and all ages. Their homes are 'open houses' which makes visitors, including their children's friends, feel welcome and relaxed.

4. **Skill** – Being the kind of people who are interested in developing their potential. They have acquired a range of intellectual and/or practical skills which help them to do so to good effect. They are always keen to learn and become more knowledgeable, accomplished and competent. Even when they are doing fairly 'menial' tasks they like to do these with finesse and proficiency. This means that they ensure that their home life as well as their working life is excellently managed.

    They are also very socially skilled, having learned, for example, how to communicate efficiently, how to be assertive and how to manage their emotions. They enjoy sharing their knowledge and skills with their children and are keen to learn new approaches, techniques and ideas from them as well.

5. **Stimulation** – Inspiring to be with as they encourage others also to use their potential and they supportively guide their children into activities and relationships which are challenging and interesting. They are keen to surround themselves and their children with resources such as materials, toys, books, music and videos which will encourage and foster enthusiasm and activity. Their energizing qualities arise from a firm foundation of positive beliefs – in themselves, other people and the world in general.

6. **Sense** – while never being stuck in a rut and always progressing, they also have both feet firmly on the ground. This means that their creativity is constructively used because their innovations and visionary projects are always 'supervised' by the practical and pragmatic side of their nature.

    They make sure that their risks and challenges have at least a 50 per cent chance of success and they always make contingency plans in case outcomes are not as successful as they hoped. They make every effort to ensure that their financial base is sound and they take as much responsibility as they can for planning for 'rainy days'. This means that they try to live within their means and do not allow themselves to get addicted to habits which over-strain their financial resources. They plan and manage life so that it is balanced and they – and the people they are responsible for – do not get over-stressed. They are committed to providing enough security and stability so their children are not constantly 'infected' with anxiety, worry and fear that their basic needs may not be met.

7. **Successfulness** – Being the kind of people who could look back on their life in old age and feel they have used it well and got the best out of their own potential. They are the kind of people who are achievers and winners because they constantly set themselves challenging but achievable goals. If they find themselves in jobs which do not allow them to progress and shine, they seek new employment to find other avenues and activities which will encourage them to thrive and prosper. Similarly, they seek relationships that positively help and do not hinder the best use of their talents and the opportunities around them. They are also able fully to appreciate, enjoy and share the personal and material rewards for their successes, so that their children grow up motivated to achieve and be similarly successful.

Now let's examine the characteristics of the 'sinners' of the parenting world. These are the kind of people whom we all want to think are very different from us because, however hard they may sometimes try, they still seem to have a negative effect on their children's confidence. I doubt very much if you are an extreme version of the sinner (because after all you *are* reading this book) – but as you read through the following list of characteristics, be honest with yourself and note whether any uncomfortable bells begin to ring.

The seven 'sinful' characteristics of 'not good-enough' parents

1. **Selfishness** – Wanting their children first and foremost to satisfy their needs (e.g. for love, fun, companionship or power and control). Directing and manipulating their children into certain activities and studies so that they (the parents) can bask in reflected glory. Not being willing sometimes to sacrifice their own comforts or pleasures for the good of their children's development.

2. **Spitefulness** – Using physical and emotional power to hurt their children, perhaps because they are envious of their potential, success or even their youth. Using their children as 'easy targets' for venting the anger and hate they feel against either themselves, other people or the world in general. Witholding positive feedback, treats or comforts because they themselves had to (and perhaps still do) manage without them. Always taking

the last word in an argument or making sure that they defeat children at their favourite game or sport. Deflating a child's pleasure in his or her success by bringing up the subject of their own superior achievements.

3. **Sanctimoniousness** – Always knowing what is best and being unable to see that anyone else's values could be worthwhile; being smugly sure about the meaning and purpose of life and not giving their children enough space to develop their own philosophies and moral codes. Unwilling to admit to mistakes even though they may be inwardly aware of their own hypocrisy and guilt; preaching but not always practising virtue.

4. **Scepticism** – Persistently putting out 'dampeners' by emphasizing what is or could go wrong, or how something could be done better. Generally suspicious of people and reluctant to trust – even themselves. Teaching their children to view the world and the future through grey-coloured spectacles.

5. **Sorrow** – Being too full of their own unresolved grief to be able to share in, and nurture, their children's natural *joie de vivre*; looking too frequently over their shoulder at the 'good old days' and the 'if onlys' of their lives; getting their children to feel they should feel sorry for them or even care for them before meeting their own needs; clinging to their own sadness and pain to such an extent that they are unable to appreciate and celebrate their children's successes and happiness fully; giving their children the message that they could make amends for the unsatisfactory nature of their parents' personalities or lives by, for example, being extra-assertive, prosperous or famous.

6. **Servility** – Being at everyone's beck and call and, as a result, getting prematurely burnt out and bitter and therefore having little or no energy to give to their children. Doing too much for their children and then wondering why they end up being held back, becoming too clingy or showing disrespect rather than gratitude.

7. **Stagnation** – Being resistant to change and new ideas. Teaching their children to 'play too safe' and go for the easy, familiar options. Giving them a lifestyle that is over-controlled by routine and regular rituals and that gives them little time and space for spontaneity and exiting new challenges. Being unwilling to try to make new friends, travel to different places or even just watch a diverse range of TV programmes in order to widen the horizons of their naturally curious children.

Of course most of us are (and will always be) an amalgam of both sinner and saint, and on some occasions we will look more predominantly like one than the other. That's fine, *as long as the mixture is a 'good-enough' blend*. However, if your children are continually receiving an overdose of the sinner part of you or experiencing a confusing curdle of messages from both, you will almost certainly be damaging their confidence to some degree or other. But, before you start reaching for the telephone numbers of psychiatrists or adoption agencies, why not try some simple self-improvement strategies?! If you take some action in any of the following five areas it can only have a positively helpful effect. So for a while take the focus of your attention off your children, turn your critical (and caring) eye inwards and work through each of these following steps:

Step 1: Become acquainted with your 'auto-parent'

'We don't see things as they are, we see things as we are.'

Anais Nin

I know that most of my own 'sins' against my children's confidence and well-being have been committed *in spite* of my good intentions. I used to hear myself saying:

'How could I have done that?'
'I didn't mean to say that.'
'I didn't realize that I was doing that.'

I was doing and saying things I would never have done or said in other relationships. Furthermore I was behaving in ways that I knew had hurt and restricted me as a child and that I had sworn no one would ever see me doing to *my* children. Why should this have been so?

The reason was that when my children were very young I was often acting in 'auto-parent' mode. Like many stressed and anxious mothers, I did not have the energy or time to think through and make conscious choices about what words and actions I would like to use, I just reacted and acted *spontaneously*. The difficulty was that my 'spontaneity' was (as is everybody's) more the product of my own experiences as a child and my cultural conditioning than of any pure and virtuous maternal instinct. When I later began to try and understand my behaviour I realized that in my parenting role I was often acting just as the people who reared me as a child behaved. This was a tremendous shock to me, because I had hitherto liked to consider myself a very different kind of mother! The hard truth I had to swallow was that, in spite of all my good intentions and studies of good child care, I was still under the powerful influence of my early role-models.

I had an unusually deprived childhood; hopefully you have more satisfactory parenting models lodged in your auto-parent. Nevertheless it may still be worth doing some serious self-reflection to enable you to make sure that, when your auto-parent is in operation (and it often has to be), it's doing the job *you* want it to do (and not, for example, the job that anyone else may have programmed it to do!) Remember that even if the parenting you experienced was 'good-enough' for you it may not be exactly right for building the confidence of your particular children. After all, some of the beliefs underlying your parents' style may simply be out of date in today's culture (e.g. the 'Spare the rod, spoil the child' variety.)

The following exercise will help you to become much more

aware of the beliefs that may have been programmed into your
auto-parent, and then replace those you want to change with
alternatives.

EXERCISE **Discovering my auto-parent**

- Read slowly through the following 'parenting messages'
  and take notice of your reaction to each. Taking each in
  turn, ask yourself:

1. Would my parents have agreed with the belief behind
   this message? Or did they act as though they agreed
   with it?
2. Did any other significant figures hold this belief dear to
   their hearts (e.g. teacher or grandparent)?
3. As a child, was my confidence positively or adversely
   affected in any way by this belief?

Children are certain cares but uncertain comforts.

Children should be seen and not heard.

You cannot put an old head on young shoulders.

The fine pullett shows excellence from the egg.

A child may have too much of his mother's blessing.

Spare the rod spoil the child.

Little things please little minds.

Soon ripe soon rotten.

- Make a list of sayings, statements or beliefs which you feel
  may have stunted the growth of your confidence. These do
  not have to be well-known like those above, they could be
  sentences or quotes which, for you, sum up the
  philosophy behind the 'faulty' messages you received
  about parenting. For example:

- 'Parents always know best.'
- 'You're just a child, you could never understand.'
- 'Boys are more important than girls.'
- 'Girls are much better at relationships than boys.'

- Show this list to your partner (or anyone else whom you may be able to talk to on the subject) and ask them to tell you whether they recognize the influence of these beliefs in the way you are bringing up your children. Ask them to help you become more aware of when their influence is operating, perhaps against your own will. Make sure that you *don't* invite unhelpful general put-downs. What you need is *specific* feedback such as:

  'I know you were very excited, but at lunchtime you were talking again way over the children's heads and Paul couldn't get a word in edgeways.' (Children should be seen and not heard.)

  'Your tone of voice sounded a bit patronizing when you were talking to Jane about her Christmas list.' (Little things please little minds.)

- Start to reprogramme your mind with alternative, positive messages. Make a list of your own beliefs about good parenting and pin these up in a prominent place. Read them frequently and affirm them by saying them out loud from time to time. (You could use the List of Rights on page 133.)

Step 2: Become aware of your wounded inner child

In the last exercise you were working on what is often referred to in the world of therapy as the *parent* part of your personality. This is the part of you that not only wants and needs to look after others, but also to judge and direct them. Now we are going to turn our attention to another part which is commonly called the *child* part. When we use this term we are usually referring either to *natural* traits which, like every child, you inherited at birth – such as:

> spontaneity, inquisitiveness, intuition, creativity, playfulness, adventurousness, sensuality, trustfulness, egocentredness

– or to *adaptive* traits which you developed in early childhood in response to the environment in which you grew up and the way your needs were (or were not) met. These might have been, for example:

> compliancy, submissiveness, helplessness, attention-seeking, manipulativeness, rebelliousness, fearfulness.

With the arrival of our own children, the *child* part of us is re-stimulated and re-energized and can, of course, be a very positive force in our parenting. I know that some of the closest 'bonding' moments I have ever had with my children have been when I have just let myself get totally absorbed in their play or their fantasy world or, in contrast, when we have wept or laughed 'uncontrollably' in each other's arms. Not only were such experiences good for my relationships with my daughters, they also were feeding and satisfying some important needs in the child part of me which craved fun and intimacy. On these occasions I would return to my adult responsibilities refreshed and invigorated.

There were also many other times when this part of me did not play such a positive role. This was when my own unmet needs from childhood were in the 'driving seat' of my unconscious. For example, because I grew up in a very insecure atmosphere, my *child's* need for 'peace at any price' overshadowed my daughter's need to learn to negotiate and argue. Also, because I had been the subject of so much bullying, I had a 'childish' urge to get revenge. So when I did let go of my pent-up anger, I could be unjustifiably petty and spiteful.

John Bradshaw, one of the leading experts in this field, explains in his book, *Homecoming*:

'. . . *when a child's development is arrested, when feelings are repressed, especially the feelings of hurt, a person grows up to be an adult with an angry, hurt child inside of him. This child will spontaneously contaminate the person's adult behaviours.*'

So, those of us who have an over-abundance of unmet needs or unresolved feelings from childhood are likely to find that from time to time our auto-parent is unconsciously being 'driven' by our *wounded inner child* which has been programmed with many self-destructive and hurtful habits and responses. As a result, we may find ourselves unconsciously driven to satisfy needs that are, in fact, incompatible, inconsistent, insatiable and in direct conflict with the development of our children's confidence.

There will, of course, be times when we are only too aware that we have behaved in a damaging, 'childish' manner and then, hopefully, most of us will quickly apologize to our children and tell them how we would have preferred to respond. Unfortunately, it is also highly likely that there will be times when we will be totally *unaware* that our wounded inner child is in the driving seat. In fact, we may be defensively convinced that

we are acting in the best interests of our child! For example:

A parent with a jealous inner child, enforcing some ridiculously oppressive curfew rule on a teenager might say –

'Your generation has no idea what the word "strict" even means. It may be hard for you to understand why I insist on this time, but I know that when you are older, you'll appreciate that it was good for you and we had your interests at heart.'

or,

A parent with an over-anxious inner child squashing a minor quarrel between two children might say –

'I'm putting you both to bed right now to save you pulling each other's eyes out.'

Such rationalizations just pour more oil on the troubled waters, because the confusion which such 'double messages' cause in the minds of our children will inhibit most of them from answering or fighting back. Instead, their self-esteem gets yet another dent as they conclude that the problem (whatever it seems to be) must be their fault. (After all, children will always strive to think the very best of their parents, even against overwhelming evidence to the contrary.)

Unless your childhood was blissfully free of hurts, disappointment and loss, the chances are that you too have a wounded inner child which could spoil your adult efforts to build your child's confidence. I've listed below some of the most common 'sabotage patterns', together with the kind of things we might be saying, or thinking, at the time. I have then noted an example of an *inner child wound* which is commonly a root cause of the damaging behaviour.

SABOTAGE	WORDS OR THOUGHTS	INNER CHILD WOUND
Over-compensation	'I'm going to make sure my children don't have to go through what I went through.'	Often the result of hurt or disappointment.
Over-dependency	'I'm sure I'm doing it wrong, I'll have to ask Jill or get a new book on the subject.'	Often a result of not having enough approval.
Inappropriate imitation	'We always did it this way when I was a child.'	Often the result of love being given too conditionally.
Over-protectiveness	'A person can't be too careful.'	Often the result of insecurity or frightening experiences or being 'smothered' with protection
Over-ambitiousness	'Only "A" grades are good enough.'	Often a result of having under-achieved as a child.
Perfectionism	'There's no point in trying if I can't do it properly.'	Often a result of not being allowed to make mistakes or take risks.
Over-seriousness	'Life is hard – the sooner my children learn that lesson the better.'	Often the result of having had to grow up too quickly.
Irresponsibility	'Let's have another drink and let fate take care of tomorrow.'	Often the result of being either over- or under-controlled as a child.

SABOTAGE	WORDS OR THOUGHTS	INNER CHILD WOUND
Revenge	'It won't do them any harm to suffer a bit – we had it a lot tougher than them.'	Often the result of emotional or physical abuse.
Bullying	'You'll do as I say or else.'	Often a result of having been hurt and deprived of reasonable rights as a child.
Inflexibility	'You've made your bed, now you have to lie in it.'	Often a result of having to come to terms with apparently unchangeable negative situations.
Uncontrolled Emotions	'I couldn't stop myself – you made me so angry.'	Often as a result of having emotions repressed and not being given advice on how to handle them.

If, after reading this list your warning bells have begun to sound, don't despair, you *can* do something to change these unhelpful patterns.

EXERCISE: **Sabotaging behaviours of my inner child**

This exercise will help you to identify your own specific sabotage habits so that you can be more on your guard, bring them into your consciousness and therefore have more control over them.

This exercise will take at the very least an hour and a half; if you can spare longer you will benefit even more from doing it. Find somewhere to sit where you can be sure of having uninterrupted peace. You will need some photos of your childhood or any significant memorabilia such as toys or books and, if possible, some relaxing music.

38

- Spend 5 to 10 minutes looking through your photos or at your objects.
- Put on the music you have chosen and spend two or three minutes making a conscious effort simply to relax. Once you feel relaxed allow your mind to 'wander through' some of the memories of your childhood. After a while, spend 20 minutes focusing your mind on some of the disappointments, hurts and losses you can either remember feeling or can imagine you must have felt. Remember that you may not be searching for major traumas, but rather a series of smaller incidents, because these together can often add up to a significant wound. If you find specific memories hard to recall, reflect quite generally on your relationships and the lifestyle or ethos of your family or school. You can make a note of these as you remember each.
- Now try to make a link between these early experiences (i.e. your inner-child's wounds) and possible difficulties you could (or indeed do) have in parenting your child in the way you would like to do. Use the list I gave on pages 37–8 as a guide, but remember that it is not an exhaustive list, so add some of your own.
- Make your own list. It might include points like these:
  'I may be too bullying because I resented my father's strictness.'
  'I could over-compensate with too much generosity because my parents were mean.'
  'I am possibly over-protective because no one protected me from being hurt.'
  'I could resent my children's freedom to have adventures because we had such a quiet, sheltered upbringing and I felt totally unprepared for the knocks and challenges you can get in life.'
  'I might get over-anxious about academic achievements because my school failed to help me realize my potential.'
  'Perhaps I'm trying to imitate my parents too much by

not letting the children "fight it out" because we were never allowed to argue at home.'
'I could over-react when the children criticize me because I was rarely allowed to speak my mind.'

- Discuss these with your partner, a trusted friend and even your children if they are old enough. Ask them to give you feedback if ever they think you are dampening your child's confidence with one of these behaviours.

Step 3 – Give some attention to your own dreams and desires

'Those who lose dreaming are lost.'

Proverb

Another not-so-obvious way in which children's confidence gets damaged is through their parents' abandonment of their own dreams. When this has happened children have very often picked up either a direct or indirect message which, in effect, says 'All I really have left in life is you and my hopes for your future.'

Children who feel they have this kind of responsibility for their parents' happiness are almost guaranteed to feel a continuous sense of failure – because however brilliant their exam results may be, however beautiful or strong they make themselves, however obedient or helpful they are, however 'nice' their friends may be, or however hard they try to smooth any troubled waters – the reality, almost inevitably, will be that Mum and/or Dad will still find life disappointing. (After all, vicarious pleasure is rarely as good as the 'real stuff'!)

Very few parents would, of course, *intentionally* 'set-up' their children for such failure, but nevertheless their self-neglect or self-sacrificing *behaviour* conveys the same message. I am sure you can think of *at least* two or three examples of happy, ambitious, talented, creative people who, since they started a family, have simply drifted into a life of child-orientated routines, rituals and conversations. I know from my own 'near-miss' experience of doing just this, that once such ruts are established it is all too easy to find ourselves literally 'living through' our children, and extremely hard to find the motivation and energy to retrieve our own ambitions.

So, to combat these seductive unconscious leanings towards letting your children take the burden of providing the bulk of your happiness, you may well be advised to check regularly that your dreams are not simmering away into the realms of oblivion on that notorious parental 'back burner'. You can start now by doing this next exercise.

EXERCISE: **Recovering my dreams**

- Spend some time getting yourself into a relaxed state in a peaceful setting.
- Close your eyes and, for at least a full five minutes, try to picture yourself in 10 years' time – leading what for *you* would be an *ideal* life. Answering the following questions might help you to get the picture.
    - where are you living and what does the house look like?
    - whom are you living with?
    - what job are you doing and what do you enjoy about it?
    - what kind of social life do you have? Any new friends?
    - what have you achieved in the last 10 years?
    - what are your plans for the next 10 years?
- Share this dream with your partner, if you have one (if not use a close friend) and then listen to his or her dream.
- 'Rewrite' your dream into one or more *achievable but ambitious goals*.
- Note down the obstacles in relation to your children which you think are standing in the way of you living your dreams. For example:
    - unreliable child care support
    - not being able to afford the fees for the course as well as paying for the children's swimming/music lessons

- 'the kids sap every ounce of my spare energy'
- 'I couldn't apply for promotion because that might mean moving the children to another area and they never settle at a new school.'
- 'I believe that it's parents' sacred duty to always put their children's needs first and I would never forgive myself if I didn't always do that.'
- 'when I think what my parents gave up for me, postponing the start of my degree pales into insignificance.'

• Using the help of your partner or a friend, critically challenge each of the obstacles you have written down. Ask yourself whether these really are immovable obstacles or whether you are, perhaps, subconsciously using the children as an 'honourable' excuse for not facing the challenge of living up to your full potential.

• Devise an *action plan*, which includes at least one step which you can take within the next two weeks, and pin this up in a prominent place. For example:
  - obtain an Open University prospectus
  - talk to other working parents about their child care
  - get some motivational and confidence-building cassettes
  - book yourself on to a time-management course
  - join the health club

• If your children are old enough, *share* your dream, goals and plans with them. You may be able to enlist their help or co-operation in some way (e.g. write out your action plan in some attractive way and then ask them to check up on you; devise a rota for cooking meals or ask them to teach you how to work the computer!) – just think what a boost that would give to their sense of self-worth!

Remember:

Confidence spontaneously flourishes in an atmosphere of excitement, happiness and success.

Step Four – Increase your knowledge about child care and development

'Knowledge is power.'

This saying holds just as true in the field of confidence-building as it does almost anywhere else. During the last 50 years, through scientific research and the rapid exchange of information and skills, the world has amassed a considerable amount of information about very many aspects of child care. This knowledge has (at least in theory!) given us more power to bring up children who are physically fit, emotionally strong and socially skilled. I have no doubt that the children whose parents have been able and willing to acquire this new wisdom are emerging into the world with many advantages that are relevant to the growth of confidence.

How to become a good-enough parent

'The longer I live the more keenly I feel that whatever was good enough for our fathers is not good enough for us.'

Oscar Wilde

Well-informed parents, who *remain* always keen and interested to learn (as opposed to the 'know-all' variety) will be better able to:

– obtain the resources which can help their children make the best use of their potential
– give a child a sense of security because they can make decisions more easily and, in terms of crisis, they will know what can or cannot be done (e.g. they will not need to keep running to the doctor or the headmaster in a panic with minor complaints)
– demonstrate the power of personal qualities such as resourcefulness and self-reliance.

It is beyond the scope of this book even to begin to summarize the vast body of relevant knowledge from the fields of child health, education and psychology, but the following exercise will highlight some of the advantages of keeping informed and help you to begin to identify some key areas in which you may wish to 'educate' yourself.

But first, some words of warning from someone who has been close to overdosing on the subject! The pool of available wisdom is so rich, varied and endlessly fascinating that there is a danger that some of the perfectionists among us could become addicted or obsessed. If you find that you are becoming so engrossed in articles on nutrition and intelligence quotients that you forget, or haven't time, to go to the market to buy fresh vegetables, or you are spending so much cash on child care books that there's none left for pantomime tickets – then you are certainly going too far! But seriously, many of us do need to remind ourselves from time to time that we are not aiming for first-class honours in parenting but merely the acquisition of 'good-enough' information. And remember, the very fact that you are reading this book indicates that you are very likely to be getting the most important aspects of your parenting right!

'No period in history has been more child-orientated than ours, nor produced parents who regard themselves as so inadequate. After generations when they could do no wrong, many parents now feel themselves incapable of doing anything right.'

David Lewis, *How to be a Gifted Parent*

Take time to read the following checklist. Make a note of any questions you are unable to answer – than (instead of burying yourself under a mountain of guilt!), consult the Action Plan Exercise on page 49.

1. Do you have adequate knowledge about child health issues?

- Are you able to help your children maintain their optimum standard of health so that they can make the best of their physical and intellectual potential?
- Are you well-informed enough to be an excellent model of how to handle health problems, illness and accidents in a calm, positive and confident manner?
- Do you know enough about the professional health services around you to be able to use these appropriately, speedily and assertively?
- On the self-help front, do you, for example, know enough about relevant issues such as:

  – nutrition (e.g. is it true that fish feeds the mind; that additives can induce hyperactivity; that vitamins enhance performance and that children must eat greens, etc.?)
  – physical fitness (e.g. do children need to do extra exercises or sport or will they be fit enough through just running off their natural energy?)
  – the symptoms of common childhood illnesses (e.g. would you panic at the sight of red blotches, or brush off meningitis as a bad cold?)
  – first aid (e.g. could your child's self-esteem take a battering through having a disfigurement or disability for

life just because you don't know how to deal with a
scald or how to handle a broken limb?)
- teeth (e.g. can you distinguish toothache from a tantrum?
Would there be a danger that you would too often treat
the two similarly just because you were not
knowledgeable enough about teething? For the sake of
your child's self-image, does research indicate that it is
worth persevering with braces for crooked teeth?)

2. Do you need to know more about education?

* Will you be able to give your children informed and
appropriate support in their educational development?
Many parents damage children's confidence by pushing
them too early to learn and do things which they are not
yet capable of doing. (e.g. Do you know at what age *most*
children should be able to start reading or understanding
abstract concepts? Are educational toys and aids worth the
money, or do children do better without them?)
* Do you know how to spot some of the major learning
difficulties? Some children's confidence is damaged because
these are noticed too late – we cannot always rely on the
schools or doctors to spot these. (e.g. Do you know what
dyslexia actually is, and what help you can get for it? Do
all schools have to offer remedial classes?)
* Do you know enough about *current* curricula, exam systems
and qualifications? I have known the confidence of many
children become damaged simply through being forced
into an inappropriate educational rut in which they have
no hope of thriving. This often happens because parents
are anxious that their children should have security in a
career, and they do not want to see their children making
the mistakes they made or which they have seen others
make, e.g. giving up certain subjects, leaving the
educational system too early, or even becoming over-

qualified! In this ever-changing field it is very important not to rely solely on our personal experience, because the routes to even the most traditionally secure careers have changed enormously over the last 20 years.

- If you are helping your children with their homework, are your methods and sources of information up-to-date or could you be confusing your child and making them more anxious? (Don't forget that many children in such a situation do *not* disclose their confusion for fear of upsetting their parents or appearing as stupid as they themselves feel.)

3. Do you know enough about behaviour difficulties?

- Are any of the following examples considered fairly 'normal' behaviours in children of a certain age? If so, *roughly* at what stage in your children's development might you expect to see each of these?

  - head-banging
  - bedwetting
  - temper tantrums
  - nightmares
  - 'seeing' ghosts
  - talking to an imaginary friend
  - refusing to be parted from a comfort blanket/teddy
  - writing on walls
  - sexual talk and behaviour
  - persistent talk about death (including their own)
  - ritualist and obsessional behaviours
  - masturbation
  - obsession with fire
  - avoidance of school (inexplicable stomach-aches?)
  - jealous behaviour
  - lying

- stealing
- experimenting with smoking/drink/drugs
• Are you clear about how you might handle such behaviour difficulties? (If not, don't despair, Chapters 5 and 11 may be of some help!)

4. Do you know where to go for professional help if you or your child needs it?

• Do you know the difference between these following professionals? If not, do you know how to find out the difference should you ever need to know?
  - paediatrician
  - child psychologist
  - child psychiatrist
  - child psychotherapist
  - child analyst
  - children's social worker
  - children's health visitor
• Do you know whether you and your children have a right to free or subsidized help from these kind of professionals?
• Do you know when and how to ask for such a service should you decide that your child ever needs it?

5. Have you enough knowledge on social dangers which your child might encounter?

• Do you know what everyday products children use for 'glue-sniffing' highs?
• Are you clear about the difference between hard and soft drugs? Would you be able to spot the symptoms in a child who might be experimenting with various drugs?
• Do you know enough about HIV and AIDS and sexually-transmitted diseases?

EXERCISE: **Action plan to upgrade my knowledge**

You may feel a bit daunted by the number of questions in the checklist you were unable to answer, but help is always at hand. To start, note down any action you may want to take in order to supplement your knowledge in each of the subject areas – for example:

- Re. education: contact or visit the local school, your local council, the library or a bookshop (see the Further Reading section) could help
- Re. health: discuss your questions with your GP; take a first-aid course, contact your local health authority for further information
- Re. law: visit the local Citizen's Advice Bureau
- Re. behaviour difficulties: enrol on an Adult Education course on the subject; discuss with your GP; join a parent network group

Finally, as I said earlier, *never* feel that you need to 'know it all', because that could be as damaging to the growth of your children's confidence as not knowing enough. What is important is that you are aware of the extent and the limitations of your knowledge and can show your children how you are prepared to make an effort to learn whatever may be helpful to them (even when they themselves may be your instructor!)

'The first step to knowledge is to know that we are ignorant.'
Lord David Cecil

Step five – Improve your ability to manage stress

Stress-management courses have now become a routine part of most training programmes in successful businesses. I am sure that the reason for this development is not that most managers and directors have suddenly become much more altruistic – they have simply learned from experience that teaching positive ways of handling stress increases efficiency! It would seem that many parents need to learn the same lesson – after all, their levels of stress often far exceed those found in the business world. Not only is the parenting role physically, emotionally and mentally demanding, it also does not appear to offer an *immediate* reward to encourage us to handle the inevitable 'downs'.

How can mismanagement of stress damage our children's confidence? I believe that there are two main ways: first when we allow ourselves to become overly stressed and therefore haven't enough patience or energy to parent in the way we know we should. For example, if we are too stressed, we:

- can't be bothered to wait all day while a child fiddles with his or her shoelaces, so we do them up
- only see the mess on the sitting room floor instead of noticing that an imaginative castle has been painstakingly constructed
- unjustly 'ground' our teenager for being late because we haven't the energy to listen to his or her reasonable explanation.

Secondly, as I indicated earlier, when overly stressed we are much more likely to slip into negative responses from our auto-parent and wounded child.

We all react to stress in individual ways, and the amount of pressure each of us can take before having a negative reaction varies enormously. Some parents might find the tantrums of one toddler too much, while others might need the screams of 10 in unison to shake their saintly equilibrium. Equally, a quick cup of tea or a walk around the garden might restore one parent to inner harmony, while another might need an hour of aromatherapy to calm her shattered nerves. Stress-management strategies and programmes must always be individually tailored; this is why I believe regular *self-appraisal* is the most important key to managing high levels of pressure effectively.

When checking ourselves over for signs of negative stress reactions we need to look objectively at each of these areas:

– our physical health
– our emotional state
– our mental functioning
– our behaviour

A quick way of doing this is to have a short list (either in our heads or on paper) of our own individual *tell-tale signs*. These are the 'symptoms' which are likely to occur when we have gone beyond our coping threshold. The reason we need to have such a list is that stress has an insidious habit of creeping up on us gradually without us realizing what strain we are under.

In order to cope with the increased pressure of stress, our bodies start producing extra supplies of adrenalin and other energy-boosting hormones. One effect of this extra 'charge' to our systems is that we feel a bit 'high' and actually experience less physical pain. So it's not surprising that over-stressed people

often do not seem to know when to say 'no' to additional pressures and appear to be unaware of their negative effects ('Yes, of course, bring along as many other children as you like – the more the merrier.') But then (surprise, surprise!) they will suddenly reach their own 'breaking point' which may manifest itself in a variety of ways, ranging from the 'blinding headache' to 'blind rage'.

The next exercise will help you to identify your own individual warning signals. These are your own personal set of symptoms which can be used as indicators that you may be on the slippery road to 'burn-out'. Once you notice them beginning to appear, you will know that this is the time to arrange some 'decompression' time to engage in some activity that will help you to unwind. Your goal must be to bring your mind and body back to a comfortable and efficient level of functioning. (For busy parents it may be over-ambitious to think that they can live in a permanent state of calm and inner harmony!). And of course, what will help *you* to relax and re-vitalize yourself will depend on your own individual personality and lifestyle. Remember, there is no magic 'cure-all' for stress – each of us has to experiment with different ways of relaxing until we find our own individual formula.

'The time to relax is when you don't have any time for it.'

Sydney Harris

EXERCISE: **My stress warning signals**

In each section below, list the symptoms which *you* are most likely to experience and notice when you are under too much pressure.

Physical signs of stress

For example: sweaty palms; breathlessness; dizziness; palpitations; indigestion; stomach cramps or 'butterflies'; nausea; shoulder, neck or back pain; muscle fatigue; pins and needles; tired eyes; humming in the ears; toothache from clenched or grating teeth; frequent urination; thrush; bladder infections; sinus problems; frequent viral infections; weight gain or loss; constipation or diarrhoea; skin problems; neuralgia;

disturbed menstrual cycle. Now list your own physical reactions to stress in the space provided.

....

....

....

Emotional signs of stress
For example: increased anxiety; being easily hurt or upset; tearfulness; irritability; depression; confusion; feelings of detachment and apathy; disorientation; boredom, humourlessness; moodiness; 'silly' guilt feelings; low self-esteem; selfishness; helplessness; paranoia; insecurity; loneliness; persistent or inappropriate anger. Now list your own tell-tale emotional signs in the space provided.

....

....

....

Mental signs of stress
For example: lack of concentration; forgetfulness; inability to think clearly; going 'blank'; making simple arithmetical mistakes; obsessional thoughts; worrying over insignificant details; mind racing from one thought to the next; inability to 'switch off' mind for relaxation or sleep. Now list your own symptoms in the space provided.

....

....

....

Behavioural signs of stress
For example: restlessness; making mountains out of molehills; 'flitting' ineffectually from one task to the next; inability to make decisions; poor planning; procrastination; poor control of finances; losing things; bumping into things; talking too much; moaning; nervous habits such as scratching or nail-biting; increased smoking, drinking or eating; insomnia; nightmares; being late; untidiness; unkempt appearance; having more arguments; outbursts of irritability or rage; reluctance to delegate; over-protectiveness; impotence; loss of libido; decrease in

assertiveness; poor communication or listening; difficulty in adapting to change. Now list your own symptoms in the space provided.

....
....
....

If you find that your symptoms of stress are appearing more and more frequently and your 'decompression activities' seem to have little or no effect, then it may be time to start doing a radical reorganization of your lifestyle and self-care habits.

Then, if you find that this doesn't work, don't resign yourself to an early grave or put the children up for auction. Resolve to do some appropriate personal development work. Use the following exercise to plan some action you may need to take in order to prevent the build-up of any unnecessary stress.

EXERCISE: **Action plan for stress prevention**

- Ask yourself if you could benefit, for example, from:
  - a more nutritious diet (to give you more energy)
  - a new exercise plan (to release built-up tension)
  - assertiveness training (to help you stand up for your rights)
  - time management (to help you organize and plan efficiently)
  - communication skills (to improve your relationships)
  - meditation classes (to revive your thinking and creative powers)
  - anxiety and anger management (to give you more emotional control)
  - budgeting (to help you take better control of your finances)
  - philosophy (to help you assess your priorities in life)
  - DIY classes (to help you be less dependent on unreliable helpers!)
  - additional friends (to help support you and have fun with)

- Now add your own ideas below:

....
....
....
....
....

Once you have learned to manage your own stress, just think what an excellent model and stress-management trainer you will be for your children!

Calmness is an essential component of confidence.

Chapter 3
Providing a helpful environment

'Home is where one starts from.'

T.S. Eliot

Preparing your home

Some of us have very little choice about the kind of home in which we bring up our children. But if we have, I feel that there are some relevant points which we should bear in mind when we are 'nest-building'. Although I am aware that most people reading this book are likely to have thought through this subject long ago and will already have prepared their homes very adequately, I have decided to include this section partly because my experience is similar to that of Dr Thomas Gordon, who writes in his book *Parent Effectiveness Training*:

'I am very often amazed at how many parents show through their attitudes and behaviour that they treat guests with far greater respect than they do their own children. Too many parents act as if children must do all the adjusting to their surroundings.'

Most of my own childhood was spent in the care of the local authority; my homes a series of impersonal institutions which

56

were created more with economy, efficiency and cleanliness in mind than the psychological needs of their inhabitants.

When at the age of 14, I was returned to my father's care and given a room of my own, I was understandably stunned and can still recall the 'dream-like' state I was in when I was taken out to choose the curtains for *my* room. Through my turbulent teenage years when I was struggling to make sense of myself and the world, that room was a safe private space to which I could always retreat. There I listened to exciting music, read books and magazines which conjured worlds I had never even imagined existed, and challenged beliefs which I had never previously had the chance to question. Also, very importantly, it was a peaceful place where I could study and at last begin to make use of some of my intellectual and creative potential. And although this 'rescue operation' came a little too late for my academic salvation at school, it did sow seeds of hope which I was eventually able to revive and cultivate nearly 30 years later! I shudder to think what other valuable parts of myself might have been lost for ever if I hadn't experienced this healing and stimulating 'nest' at that critical time in my psychological development.

Money can, of course, be an important factor in 'nest-building' (after all, it did buy the extra space for privacy which I so cherished as a teenager), but it is important to remember that environments can also be restricting even when finances appear to be 'unlimited'. Particularly through my confidence-building work I have met many people who have felt that their childhood environments had been as inhibiting as mine, even though they were brought up in comparative luxury. Their difficulties seem to have arisen from the fact that their homes were designed more with the glances of admiring neighbours in mind rather than the needs of spirited and inquisitive children.

So let's now look at some of the main factors we need to take into consideration when we are planning a home that will help, or at least not hinder, the development of a child's confidence.

Safety and security

Ideally, children need an environment which allows them to explore freely and experiment with their innate sense of adventure. In the average modern-day home their intrepidness will, of course, frequently need curbing, but nevertheless we should try to ensure that their first few years of exciting exploration should not be marred by encountering unnecessary dangers and restrictions. I have had quite a number of clients whose confidence was severely damaged because they had accidents (all avoidable) which defaced or disabled them – and damaged their self-image. I have met even more people whose self-esteem was seriously dented because the labels 'clumsy', 'careless', 'silly' or 'stupid' were fed into their 'psychological CVs', simply because they:

– broke a precious object from a temptingly placed shelf
– threw an important paper onto an open fire
– drank some forbidden liquid from a bottle which was not child-proofed
– lost Mum's purse from her open handbag
– shaved the dog with Dad's accessible razor
– ran out into the road from an unfenced garden!

Taking the position of a constantly hovering hawk, or continually shouting 'No, not there' or 'No, not that' is not only exhausting but conditions our children to be more inhibited and fearful than they need to be.

Encouragement and independence

Children need an environment in which it is possible for them to do things for themselves without too much frustration when they are ready and able to do so. Not many of us can afford

purpose-built nurseries and low-level furniture, but most of us can make small alterations which will greatly simplify our children's environment and encourage them to be more independent. (For example, low level hooks for coats and showers; accessible cupboards and unbreakable crockery.)

Another issue with regard to this factor can, of course, be the geographical position of the house. I have met many people who said they felt that their social development was hindered because their childhood home was too isolated or too far from their friends and their school. Especially as they get older, children need ready access to stimulation and friendship outside the narrow confines of their family home. Children who are isolated can feel different and 'left-out' and can also miss out on having enough opportunities to *practise* their social skills.

Stimulation

Although it is our job as parents always to focus on providing a *home* rather than a school, our children's confidence will be encouraged if we have taken care to arrange at least part of the house or garden in such a way that it stimulates them to learn and experiment creatively with their individual talents and interests. This usually means having somewhere they can, if they wish, be 'messy' and make a noise (right through to their teenage years!). This special place is likely to be filled with objects such as appropriate toys, computer, books or magazines, musical instruments or materials which will encourage our children to 'have a go' on their own.

Not only is it important for children's 'special areas' to be stimulating but also the other parts of the home where they are likely to spend time. *Family* sitting rooms, for example, can be furnished in a way that encourages all its members to feel at home there and use it to chat, pick up a book or magazine or play a game – and not just stare silently together at the TV! These communal areas are the cradle of a child's developing social skills and, of course, although I know that the people who inhabit them are more important than the fixtures and fittings, it is important that surroundings do encourage a child to feel *wanted* and *relaxed* – and not just an untidy, noisy intruder who is a threat to pristinely polished tables or precious Persian rugs! I am sure, like myself, you must be able to recognize the strangling effect that just walking into certain rooms has on you even now as a fully grown adult. This is exactly the feeling many of my clients recapture when we replay scenes set in their childhood homes.

Personal involvement

'Home was a beautiful house and an immaculate garden but it was always my parents' house. I never wanted to bring anyone home, so I stopped going to other people's houses. I became very isolated and shy.'

— participant on a confidence-building course

Contrast this by no means unique experience with that of a confident son of a friend, who recently asked his parents —

'What happens Mum when I am 18, do I leave this house or do you?'
— Tom, aged 10

Of course children shouldn't be led *mistakenly* on purpose into thinking that their parents' house is theirs for the asking when it plainly is not. But neither is it good for the development of their confidence to be brought up in an environment which makes them feel like an unwelcome temporary guest. While children are young I feel that it is very important that they feel the same sense of belonging which Tom obviously feels in his parents' house.

One way to help children feel at home in their surroundings is gradually to encourage them to become part of the decision-making which shapes *their* environment. Allowing a child to help choose, for example, the way the house is decorated or to have an opinion on the kind of house you buy or rent, can also strengthen their self-esteem, build up confidence in their own taste and develop their skills of negotiation.

Of course, there are some obvious restrictions to applying this kind of philosophy in practice (not least the financial ones), but it is nevertheless important to bear in mind that a child's home often feels like an extension of him- or herself. And rightly or wrongly, children do often judge themselves by it and are likely to be judged by it. If their home feels special because they have helped to create it, this will help them also feel a little more special.

In addition to strengthening their inner confidence, a home that feels very personal to a child will also be one which he or she will love to invite friends and visitors to share, and so there is likely to be much more opportunity to build up those important outer skills which oil the wheels of hospitality and friendship.

Privacy

Allowing children some private space, especially as they get older, will also help reinforce their self-respect. Of course not all children can (or would want to) have a room of their own, but

I doubt if there is one who wouldn't benefit from having at least some section of a room to consider his or her own. Failing this, a private drawer or cupboard will, in a very concrete way, symbolize for children the importance of their own individuality.

Finally, whatever form the home environment may take, children should take as much responsibility as they are capable of for its maintenance and upkeep. Not only do they have to learn that there are hygienic, economic and organizational benefits to taking good care of their living space, but they also need to be able to *feel* the self-worth which accompanies the satisfaction of looking after our environment. I know how hard it is, in the real world, to persevere with rules and rotas on house-care, but before giving up try the tips and strategies in Chapter 4.

EXERCISE: **Home-check**

- Using the headings in the last section as a checklist, reflect on your experiences of home as a child. Did the environment in which you lived have any impact on the development of your confidence?
- Make a note of anything you need to do, or add, to your current home which will:

  a) reinforce an atmosphere of safety and security
  b) make it more 'user-friendly' for your children
  c) allow more space for creative play and pursuits
  d) help it become a more intellectually and socially stimulating environment
  e) make the home feel more personal for your children
  f) give your children more opportunity for privacy

'A good-enough environment starts with a high degree of adaptation to individual infant needs.'

D.W. Winnicott

Chapter 4
Being a good-enough family

'I blame the family – she was always an outsider.'

'It's not surprising he's in a shell – you can cut that family atmosphere with a knife.'

'What hope was there for her to feel successful, growing up in such a competitive family?'

'That family think they are a cut above the rest of us – those poor kids are going to grow up really funny. They're kept cooped up and are never allowed to play out or go to the shops. Even going swimming has to be a major family outing.'

These are not professional psychological assessments – they are remarks which I have overheard in the street or on a train. They are not unusual – in fact, I think a skilled eavesdropper like myself could fill a book with such observations in less than a week!

But even if it is now commonly accepted that family life can have a devastatingly negative effect on the development of a child's inner and outer confidence, are most people equally as knowledgeable about the qualities required to have a *positive* effect?

Most of us carry around in our minds a rather vague image of a 'happy family' which is mostly based on an amalgam of impressions from our own personal experience and what we see in the media. But I believe that when we are struggling with the frustrations and tensions of everyday life, it is more helpful to have a clear picture of the kind of ideal family that *we* would like to provide. This picture can give us a framework of standards which can help us to judge whether or not we are achieving our aim. This is important because most people are particularly blind when it comes to spotting the weaknesses in their own family. In fact, someone once defined the family as: 'The ties that blind'. A somewhat cynical definition perhaps, but certainly one which helps to remind us that we often cannot see the mote in our own family's eye. Our keenness to be perfect parents and the subsequent guilt when we find ourselves falling short of our ideal raises our psychological defences and clouds our objectivity!

It can be equally difficult for outside observers to spot trouble. Virginia Satir, a renowned family therapist, says:

'Family life is like an iceberg. Most people are aware of only about one-tenth of what is actually going on – the tenth that they can see and hear – and often they think that is all there is.'

And of course, with regard to confidence-building in children it is usually what is under the tip of the iceberg that counts! I have found that some of the most damaging families have been those which appeared on the surface to be both happy and faultless in their functioning. It was their 'hidden agenda' which was doing the damage to the children's self-esteem and holding them back from developing their social skills. Here are some examples, which you may also recognize from your own observations:

- saying 'We love all our children and treat them all equally' when in fact one child is encouraged unconsciously to become the family scapegoat (he or she is always the one who has the accidents, illnesses or gets into trouble).
- claiming to be a very liberated non-sexist family (encouraging the girls to do science and the boys to wash up) but rewarding the girls with more attention and compliments when they show traditional 'feminine ' behaviours such as nurturing and 'being good' and allowing the male parent to wield the most real power.

– saying 'As long as our children are happy, that's all that counts. We won't mind what job or career they have or whom they marry' but taking great pride in the family tradition that every new generation produces a doctor or someone to carry on the family business. Alternatively, the hidden agenda may surface when the children start to bring home the 'wrong kind of friend'.

So, it is not good enough just to *feel* like a happy, well-meaning and encouraging family. If we want to be sure that our family life is not subtly undermining the development of our children's confidence we need, from time to time, to try and make a more *objective* assessment of how we are functioning as a unit. You could start by taking an emotional step outside your family for a moment and asking yourself the questions below. It will be very helpful if you can share your thoughts with other members of your family or someone who knows your family well. If you have a partner who shares the parenting with you, you could, of course, both read through this section and complete the exercise at the end of the chapter together.

1. Objectives and goals – shared and explicit?

We are all aware that the role of the family in Western society has undergone a radical change during this century. In fact, the actual word 'family' is no longer used to define just a group of people who are tied together by blood, marriage or adoption. It is also used to describe all sorts of other variations of small groups of people who live together without genes or a legal contract binding them together for a lifetime. One of the effects of living in this period of rapid change to the concept of 'the family' is that many parents are not clear about the aims and purpose of their 'family life' and, as a result, their children suffer from living in an atmosphere of confusion.

The aims of families can vary enormously. For example, the

goal of some may be simply to provide a shelter and nourishment for family members until they are capable of fending for themselves, while others will have moral control and guidance as primary objectives. As far as children's confidence is concerned, what is important is that these aims are *honestly* and *openly* acknowledged, and that there is some firm area of *agreement* on the primary aims between *any parent figures* who may be involved (these could include, for example, mothers-in-law and the child-minder).

It is also important that any goals you do set together are realistic. Over-ambitious goals, however worthy, can feed feelings of low self-esteem, guilt and worthlessness. Here are some examples which you may recognize.

Goal A: To create a deep bond of love, friendship and loyalty between family members so that they can support each other through 'thick and thin' for the duration of their lives.

(An unrealistic goal because each member is an individual who may or may not be on the same temperamental, ethical or intellectual wavelength as other members of the family)

Goal B: To produce children who will grow up to be adults who have 'worthwhile' careers.

(Unrealistic if only because there may be some disagreement about the definition of 'worthwhile' or because the country may be plunged into recession and any job hard to come by!)

Goal C: For all the children in the family to play a musical instrument.

(Perhaps unrealistic if the children are tone deaf or the violin teacher is incompetent or has been made redundant!)

Finally it is important to watch out for the unacknowledged objectives which may be lurking within your professed goals and are difficult to admit even to yourself. Common examples of these are:

– wanting a family which is balanced in terms of gender
  (Can be tough on the child who turns out to be the 'wrong'
  sex.)
– producing the ideal happy family which will be living proof
  (to your father/mother-in-law/sister/brother etc.) of how
  much better a parent you are than they were or are
  (Can be tough on the children who are expected to be
  people they are not when certain others are around!)

2. Values – shared or conflicting?

The confidence of so many children is damaged because they are
simply confused about the family's values. For example, they may
do something they think will please their parents and be very

hurt and saddened when they find that they get a surprisingly negative reaction.

The basic values of each family member should, as with objectives, be openly acknowledged – not only so children have a clear idea of what is 'right' and what is 'wrong' (remember the foundations of inner confidence discussed in Chapter 1) but also so that family rules can be easily identified, challenged and renegotiated when necessary. This becomes particularly important as the child begins to see alternative values in other families, and is *vital* when the child starts seriously to test out his or her own values in adolescence.

Although a family's values are essentially taught by example, it is also important that they are sometimes discussed and explained to children in terms which they understand. 'Honesty', for example, might have an obvious meaning for an adult but is not such a crystal-clear concept for a child who lives in a world of make-believe or who sees family members continually co-operating with one another's 'white lies' ('Be an angel and tell her I'm not in!').

3. Rules – commonly accepted and made explicit?

Every family needs at least a minimum number of rules, if only so that they can live safely and harmoniously under the same roof. The main problems with family rules as they affect children's confidence are:

– children often first get to know of a rule's existence only when they unknowingly break it (e.g. the unwritten rule 'Everyone over 5 years old clears up his own mess when he spills a drink' is first heard of when they meet the angry question 'Why haven't you wiped up that mess yet?')
– children often get caught in the cross-fire between two conflicting family rules. Sometimes, if a disagreement over 'rules' is being used to fuel a conflict in the parents'

relationship, then the child may be even more emotionally damaged because she may feel (rightly or wrongly) that her needs (as well as the family's rules!) have less priority than her parents' need to score points over each other.

4. Roles and responsibilities – clear and just?

'Every social group, no matter what its size, must establish patterns of authority and delegate power, status, and responsibilities to its members.'

Stanley Coppersmith

Just as the general role of the family within society is changing, so are the roles of its members in its day-to-day operation. Once again these will vary within each family and may change frequently according to the family's developing needs and abilities.

Much emotionally damaging friction could be avoided if these roles and responsibilities were openly and regularly negotiated. For example, couple counselling often reveals that men and women carry around in their heads very different perceptions and expectations concerning the role and responsibilities of 'new men' and 'liberated women'. When feelings of disappointment and irritation inevitably surface, it is often the children who are the first to suffer. First, they may be used unconsciously as instruments of 'revenge' ('I may not be the perfect "new" husband/wife/lover, but I bet I can be a better parent – just watch!') Secondly, because they are so powerless and needy children often become innocent targets when pent-up frustration and irritation are looking for an outlet.

Similarly, family counselling often reveals that parents and children often have been carrying around in their heads different expectations about the children's role and responsibilities within a family ('Older children should always protect and help with the younger ones' conflicting with 'No child should be expected to do a parent's job.')

A laissez-faire arrangement is not, of course, the only alternative to allowing gender or age to determine how authority and responsibility is divided among family members. Like many successful modern teams and partnerships in other spheres, we *can* choose to negotiate democratically appropriate and fair 'job descriptions' for each family member which take into account their individual strengths, weaknesses, age and capabilities. But, of course, because the children in the family 'team' are developing and changing so fast, we must remember to review and update the 'job descriptions' very frequently. (I suppose the perfect parent would never hear that familiar cry 'I'm not a baby anymore, you know!')

5. Communication – effective and sufficient?

Communication almost inevitably presents problems for families, if only because they contain a mix of generations. Clearly, in those that also contain a mix of gender there is an increased risk of faulty transmission!

Another important problem which we have already noted is that, when we are operating within our families, we are often acting in our auto-pilot mode and may not be as fully in control of the signals we are sending out as we may like to think we are.

It is therefore extremely important to check out regularly that messages between our family members are being correctly heard. (I believe this is one of the most important but frustratingly difficult responsibilities of parenting.) Once again, the way each family and each of its members communicates will be unique. Some will use a lot of words to convey messages to each other, some will use more body signals, others will rely heavily on actions and some will even use the written word. No method is innately better than any other if it is fully understood by both the sender and the receiver.

In respect of children's growing confidence, there are some particular questions about your family's communication that it would be helpful to ask.

a) Are we routinely checking that messages are being received and understood? (You could do this by asking those of 'the receiving end' people, particularly children to repeat back in their own words what has just been said.)

b) Are we allowing enough *time* for leisurely uninterrupted discussions and casual chats between us all, or have we drifted into the habit of talking as we pass on the stairs or taking breath between the adverts on TV?

c) Are any of the children being unfairly used as message carriers or even go-betweens within the family?

d) Are we paying attention to the non-verbal messages as well as the verbal ones?

   This is particularly important within our families because the more intimately we know each other the more we tend to rely on non-verbal communication, and we also tend to develop our special non-verbal cues and codes which only another adult or near-adult family member would understand. For example, some everyday actions can have significant hidden meanings. (Taking a cup of tea up to the bedroom could mean 'I'm upset and I want to be on my own.' / Not going to a wedding could indicate 'I disapprove of this wedding.' / Giving flowers could mean 'I have a guilty conscience.')

   On the other hand, some adults who are so used to communicating every important message with words may simply overlook the messages that their relatively inarticulate children are trying to convey through facial expressions, behaviour or even play.

e) Do we have a regular meeting 'time and space' when everybody is likely to be present and problems and issues affecting the whole family can be freely discussed? (This is often a particular meal but beware of making the discussion too formal – some family meals can be stressful enough for children!)

f) Is everybody keeping others informed about their 'diary'? (Information about who is in and out for meals, who needs lifts, etc. can be kept in a communal diary or calendar.)

g) Is there too much reliance on 'mind-reading'? ('I thought you would like to . . .; You didn't seem that keen so . . .')

Within the 'happy family' myth there seems to lurk a belief that if we really love someone, we ought to be able to know what he or she wants or is feeling. Many people have told me how difficult this was for them as children, because they felt that they were never able to be the accomplished mind-readers people expected them to be.

h) Are we giving each other enough positive feedback? (See Chapter 6).

i) Are we encouraging direct and honest negative feedback? (See Chapter 6).

j) Are we showing respect for each other's individual style and method of communicating?

Even though most families develop a common style of communicating, most will still need to make allowances for personality, gender and age. For example, I have known a number of children whose confidence was undermined because they were teased or reprimanded for using the local or school accent, instead of the family one.

k) Do we resolve our differences openly and assertively, or do negative feelings get swept under the carpet?

Another misleading idea about the 'happy family' is that arguing is bad, especially for the children. I am convinced that arguments are both an inevitable and *essential* part of family life. Moreover, they provide a safe opportunity for children to experiment with ways to stand up for their rights, beliefs and needs. In Chapter 13 we shall be looking at ways of handling conflict with children, but for the moment let's just remind ourselves that it is by watching the people they love handle their differences that children learn their most basic attitudes and responses to conflict. Within the family they can also learn through watching and experiencing that it is not necessarily just 'winning' that boosts confidence but also successful negotiation and mutually satisfying compromise.

6. The outside world — enough contact with it?

Because so many parents are now working and leading very busy and stressful lives, home often becomes a place of retreat and they feel themselves becoming very protective of their 'sanctuary'. Children, on the other hand, need to have a family which is not isolated from the world they will be expected to join when they are adults.

Ask yourself if your family:

- is providing a good-enough model of how to live companionably and co-operatively with your local community?
- is playing a *significant* role in shaping the wider world around them, and not being just a powerless cog in a machine that they feel is running riot all around them?
- welcoming enough to a wide range of visitors?
- spending enough time together *outside* its own four walls?

EXERCISE: **Family check-over**

This exercise should ideally be completed with your partner, if you have one, so it has been written assuming that you will be doing this. If your partner is unwilling or you are a single parent, do the exercise on your own but discuss your results with a friend.

Before completing each task, it may help to re-read the relevant section above.

- Each of you should make a list of the three most important aims of your family.
- Compare, discuss and compile a joint list of objectives.
- Ask yourselves if these objectives and aims are:
  1. realistic and fair
  2. openly acknowledged, and not buried under a mountain of 'hidden agendas'

3. communicated to all relevant people such as other
   parent figures and older children
- Repeat this exercise, focusing on your values
- Make a list of the family rules and, as is appropriate to
  their age, discuss these with your children, giving them
  the opportunity to challenge, question and help revise the
  list.
- Write down a short description of each individual's roles
  and responsibilities within the family. Share these with
  your children if they are old enough.
- Agree three changes you would like to make which could
  improve your family's communication with each other.
- Ask yourselves if there is anything more you would like to
  do to increase your family's involvement with the outside
  world (either in the immediate community or the world at
  large).

Finally, be careful not to get too serious about it all – the family
must be above all a relaxed, fun-loving group which children who
are spreading their wings will *want* to return to for some support
and some laughter.

> *One would be in less danger*
> *From the wiles of a stranger*
> *If one's own kin and kith*
> *Were more fun to be with.*
>
> Ogden Nash

Part 2

Laying the foundations of inner confidence

Chapter 5
Help your children to love themselves

Let's begin by reminding ourselves of the four main hallmarks of inner confidence:

- Self-love
- Self-knowledge
- Clear goals
- Positive thinking

Each of these qualities can be nurtured and/or substantially diminished by our attitudes and actions as parents. In this chapter we will look at practical ways in which we can use our substantial power and influence to help our children to feel not only good about themselves but also optimistic about what the world has to offer them.

I shall discuss each of these qualities in turn over the next four chapters, but you will probably notice that there are many areas that overlap. This, of course, means that when we are taking action in one area, we are most likely to be having a strengthening effect on others at the same time. I hope this awareness might help you to work at a gentle, step-by-step pace through this section, and not feel that you have to do everything at once! I would suggest, for example, that you could concentrate on thinking about, discussing and working on one of these four fundamental areas per week, and then return to each as and when you need to. These foundations need to last a lifetime, and so they will have to be built of sturdy, substantial psychological stuff.

In this chapter we will look at ways in which you can encourage your children to have a deep, lasting sense of their own worth, which means that they will not only feel inwardly good but will also show respect for themselves by treating themselves *as well* as they would treat anyone else whom they may happen to love.

We have already noted that the most powerful way of helping children to love themselves is by example. The second most powerful way is to take active steps to ensure that we *actively* build self-esteem and ensure that we do not discourage its natural growth. This precious psychological quality is perhaps the most essential ingredient of inner confidence. Not only does it help children feel good about themselves, but it almost certainly improves their chances of making the best of their potential and helping them withstand stress.

The press is often filled with stories of how more and more children are cracking under the strain of exams, with school and university medical and counselling services stretched to their limits. In commenting recently on this phenomena, the University of Oxford's welfare officer said, 'the people who cope best are those who have a strong sense of their personal worth.' So, instead of engaging in endless exhausting battles over unfinished homework and inadequate revision, many parents could perhaps be of more help if they work on helping their children develop and maintain this sense of self-worth!

What you can do to build children's self-esteem

'It is the child's feeling *about being loved or unloved that affects how he will develop.'* (my italics)
Dorothy Briggs, *Your Child's Self-Esteem: The Key to His life*

Say that you love them

It is fairly common knowledge nowadays that children learn to love themselves first and foremost through the *experience* of being loved and appreciated by their parents. Every therapist meets a small minority of people who have been tragically born to parents who, for different reasons, were not able to give them this very precious psychological gift. But, very much more frequently, we hear comments such as these:

'I didn't know my father liked me until I was 35 – and then it was my sister who told me.'

'I suppose my Mum must have loved us because she was always doing so much for us. But, I can't say for certain because she never said she did.'

And, although I have heard thousands of such reflections, each new one stirs great feelings of sadness in me. Missed opportunities like these become no less painful for being so common, and clearly the emotional handicapping of these people was so unnecessary. After all, these parents did love their children, but because they didn't communicate their feelings much of their confidence-building power was tragically wasted.

So it's not enough to feel love for our children, however deep, abiding and pure we know it to be. We need to **express this love clearly and frequently**. We must never assume that our children can read our hearts.

When we are expressing our love we need to be aware that children are more likely to understand and accept our messages if we use language which is:

1. **Direct** – e.g. 'I love you' rather than 'Mummy loves you.'
2. **Appropriate** – e.g. a style of communication which feels comfortable for you and makes allowances for your child's age and personality. We can actually do damage to a child's self-esteem if our message embarrasses either of us. Some adults and some children (especially as they get older) may prefer to express their love privately or even through the written word.

Explain why you like them

Although we all like to hear generalizations about ourselves which tell us that we are 'wonderful' or 'nice' or 'special' – don't we feel an even greater glow of satisfaction and pride when such appreciations are backed up with specific reasons which explain why people think we are so brilliant?

So when you are appreciating your children, always try to use *specific* examples of the qualities you admire and enjoy (e.g. 'I love your sense of fun,' 'I like the way you always notice when someone is sad or upset' or 'I really admire your creativeness.')

Emphasize the unconditional nature of your love and care

This usually means telling a child clearly that you will always love him, even if you are sometimes cross with him, either because perhaps you do not like certain behaviour or you are simply over-tired. It also means checking out that your child has not picked up the impression that there are strings attached to your commitment to loving and caring for him. Many children honestly believe that their parents' love will dry up if they do not get six exam distinctions, or become captain of the swimming team – even though this belief may be far from the truth.

A few years ago, I myself learned the hard way how this kind of misunderstanding can easily take place. When our family moved house, we rented a flat for my 17-year-old daughter for a year, so that she could complete her education at the same school. During the first couple of months I noticed that there was an awkwardness and tension between us that had not been there before, and I felt that my efforts to give her support and encouragement were being rebuffed. At first I assumed that this might be because she felt rejected or frightened, but in the aftermath of an uncomfortable row it emerged that she had neither of these feelings. Instead, it emerged that she was harbouring a much-mistaken belief that I would stop funding her flat if she didn't give a continual demonstration of total maturity and perfect housekeeping! I was so horrified that I gave her a written and signed declaration that (dead or alive!) I would ensure that her flat was paid for until her education was completed.

Although I would certainly prefer never to have had that misunderstanding, I was pleased that my daughter eventually was able to disclose her fear, because we were able relatively quickly to come to a resolution. But, of course, an ideal parent would not wait for children to declare their misconceptions, they would avoid them happening in the first place!

Share the positive effects your children have on your life

Make a point of letting your children know what a positive difference to the quality of your life their very existence has made. If you do find yourself sharing the hassles and problems as well with them, always try to balance these with a positive statement which indicates that they *are* worth the trouble. Many people I meet spent their childhood feeling inwardly haunted either by the pain their birth caused their mother, or by the strain they put on the family's budget, or the worry they piled on their over-stressed father.

So don't keep it a secret if, for example, your children have helped you to see the world through exciting new eyes, or given you an experience of deep mutual love and trust that you value above all else. They need to be told that they are worth any amount of trouble.

Regularly meet them on their level

It is important to do this both physically and intellectually. Although most people know that they should squat rather than bend down to talk to a child, ask yourself honestly if you do this enough. It is particularly important to do this when your child may have some anxiety about what you are saying, but it is also good to do it when you are just having fun together. By altering your physical position you are sending out a very powerful message to your child which is letting her know that she is worthy of your empathy and special consideration.

It is also important to make some allowances for children's intellectual level of operating. This doesn't mean that you have to learn a different language for every developmental age, but simply take care not to bombard them with adult jargon and concepts before they have the intellectual capacity to cope with them. If you are not sure what kind of language is appropriate for their age group, why not make an extra effort to watch some of their TV programmes or look at some of their favourite books, while keeping an eye on the style of communication the 'experts' have used? (It may also help to take a look at the developmental guide on page 14). Don't forget that you can also check with them from time to time that they understand you fully by asking them to repeat back to you what you have just said.

Encourage self-care and self-nurturing

I have found that one of the most effective ways for adults to boost their own flagging self-esteem is to suggest that they give themselves a strong dose of self-nurturing. Very often this suggestion is met at first with puzzlement: 'What do you mean?' The very idea of engaging in a programme of activities specifically designed to help them feel good about themselves is foreign to them because as children they were not taught either directly or by example how to nurture themselves. As a result they have developed many habits which are in essence self-destructive, if only by default (e.g. persistently going to bed too late, eating the wrong food, not getting enough exercise, not giving themselves time to relax and recover after a stressful or tiring experience, etc.). We need to teach our children from as early an age as is possible how important it is to *demonstrate* self-love to ourselves by taking good care of both our bodies and minds, and not to let ourselves be taken over by bad habits which could ultimately destroy our self-respect.

Discourage self-put-downs

When your children begin to knock their own self-esteem (as they inevitably will at a depressingly early age, because of the culture that surrounds them), you can gently point out the self-put-down and maybe suggest a way of rephrasing their feelings. For example:

Your daughter – 'What a stupid girl I am, look what I . . .'

You – 'Don't call yourself stupid, because you're not, are you? Instead you could just say – "I'm fed up because I've . . ."'

Let yourself be helped – especially by your children's strengths

As anyone who has been unemployed or incapacitated for any length of time knows, feeling that we can be useful to others, particularly to those we care about, is essential for self-esteem. It may be useful to remind yourself of this fact when you are tempted to refuse or not ask for help from your children, either because it's quicker to do something yourself or because you don't want to break up 'a happy game' or be 'a burden'.

Although children will have to learn that there are many boring and unsatisfying jobs to do in life, it is still worth trying to find additional tasks which may be a particularly satisfying way for each individual child to be of help. Our self-worth is always given an even bigger boost if, in the process of helping, we are using and building on our particular strengths. You could, for example, get an especially creative child to decorate a table or help re-design a room, or an especially logical one to count your change or reorganize a cupboard or devise a family rota.

Demonstrate your trust by not intervening

Letting children get on with an activity or task by themselves, whether it is building a sandcastle or doing a maths project, can be an important non-verbal way to communicate your respect. Often parents unintentionally give their child's self-worth a knock by rushing in with unnecessary help when they see a child struggling or getting something wrong. So before giving help or advice, always ask yourself if your *children* really need it, or if it would be better for the growth of their self-esteem to learn to take pride in their *current* potential. Remind yourself that children, like adults, take a greater pride in finding out how to do something by themselves (often through the process of making mistakes) than if they have been directly taught the skills or art.

Similarly, when a child is talking over a problem or concern, you can convey your acceptance simply by *listening* while he expresses his feelings, doubts and dilemmas. If you rush in too early with reassurances ('You'll feel different tomorrow . . .'), or unnecessary advice ('You ought to . . .'), you can unintentionally convey to a child a message that he is not OK. Often it is more affirming for a child if you respond with *silence* and just a hug. Alternatively, you could use one of the Active Listening techniques – another important social skill which we will be looking at in Chapter 9.

Prove that you care by being generous with your 'quality time'

'Quality time' is the term that is now commonly used to refer to those periods when our *whole* attention is devoted to the psychological, emotional and intellectual needs of our children (as opposed to their basic physical care). If you have very young children who are requiring vast amounts of your time to provide them with good food, clean nappies and a hygienic, efficient home – and you have a demanding job as well, I realize that this kind of time will be in very short supply. However short in supply it may be, try to make a regular and immovable slot in your diary for some quality time, because it is one of the most powerful tools you will ever have to affirm your children's sense of their own worth.

Make it clear to your children that this is their special time with you and that it is very precious, even though it may not be as long as either of you would like. If you do plan to do an activity together make sure that it is one which *they* enjoy or have an interest in. Within reason, allow your children to decide how this time is spent. My experience is that given the choice children usually choose very simple (and inexpensive) ways of passing the time with their parents.

Apportion your time according to each individual's needs

If you have more than one child, it is important to try to spend some quality time with each one *individually*, but also to remember that you do not have to divide your time up absolutely equally all the time! It is much more sensible to apportion your energy according to your children's *needs* at any given time. It is a common misunderstanding that we will damage a child's self-worth if we appear to be spending *more* time and energy on her brothers and sisters – or, indeed, on anyone else. In fact, family life provides the ideal opportunity to teach children the important humanitarian lesson that, although all human beings are equally *worthy*, they do not all require the same amount of support and attention. And, of course, as long as children have a strong foundation of inner confidence their self-esteem can indeed be *strengthened* by being given the opportunity to be generous and considerate towards others whose need is greater than theirs.

Be protective and angry on their behalf when they meet injustice

Although children's rights now appear to be becoming more and more protected in our society, it is still likely that your children will meet up with some kind of injustice or abuse which they will be too small or powerless to fight against themselves. Just in the course of their everyday lives they could, like many other children, be:

– bullied by jealous older children
– ridiculed or put down by a thoughtless or interfering relative
– inappropriately punished by a teacher
– aggressively shoved aside in a supermarket queue
– unfairly discriminated against in a recreation centre
– short-changed or given damaged goods in a shop

What would you do in any of these situations – most of the time? Of course your response will depend on the age of each of your children and the individual circumstances surrounding each event, but it will also be influenced by:

a) Your parenting philosophy and general attitudes (e.g. 'That's life. I believe children should learn to stand up for themselves – you learn from experience how to fight your own battles' or 'Bullies need a taste of their own medicine' or 'Children should be protected at all costs')

b) Your ability to manage your own anger (e.g. 'If I intervene, I just lose my cool and make things worse' or 'I wouldn't know what to say' or 'I'm not going to let this pass, it will happen again. I am going to write a strong letter.'

In relation to your child's worth, the most important point to remember is that *it is important for you as a parent to do something.*

Alice Miller, a renowned therapist and writer on child abuse, has recently made us much more aware of the fundamental psychological damage which can be done to a child's self-image if someone does not protectively rise to that child's defence. She believes (as indeed I do) that children can heal emotionally from all manner of hurt and injustice if they are psychologically rescued by what she calls an 'enlightened witness'. In other words, they need someone who is stronger and more powerful than themselves to:

1. let them know that they feel *angry* on their behalf
2. assure them that what happened was *not fair*
3. assure them that it was not their fault (note that most children will automatically think it is their fault if the perpetrator of the hurt is someone whom they love and need)
4. allow them the right to feel and express their feelings
5. take protective or defensive action on their behalf or help them to do so themselves.

And, of course, the ideal person to play the role of 'enlightened witness' to a hurt or abused child is a parent. So even if you cannot, or choose not to fight their battle for them, at the very least give your children's self-esteem a boost by letting them know how protective and outraged you feel on their behalf. You need to make sure that they know that they have a *right* to get

support until they are able to defend themselves. (Without this right they are much more likely to keep any more serious abuse which they encounter a secret.)

As children get older you will, of course, teach them appropriate self-protection strategies so that they can, whenever possible, defend themselves. (See Chapter 10).

Choose your words carefully

All parents say things they are ashamed of from time to time. Most of us have a stock of 'put-downs' programmed into our auto-parent, and we are bound to use some of them when we are under stress, *but* we can train ourselves to use many fewer on an everyday basis simply by becoming more aware of what we are saying. Remember that the odd remark may not do much harm, but if a child is drip-fed with put-downs they will infiltrate his or her basic self-image.

Use the following chart as a quick reference guide – even more important, make a note of your own 'favourite' phrases (i.e. the things you habitually say which you wish you didn't!). Give the list to the family and ask them to tell you when you use any of the phrases so that you will have an opportunity to undo the damage by *apologizing* and getting some *practice in rephrasing* what you wanted to say in language which doesn't damage self-esteem. (Later chapters will give you a guide on more assertive and constructive language which can be used in most situations.)

Language that can diminish self-esteem

Some of the following phrases could be used quite innocently, so remember that the clue to a put-down or destructive comment is often found in the *non-verbal language* which accompanies it (e.g. a sarcastic or patronizing smile, an aggressive tone, martyr's sigh, raised eyebrows, shake of the head, etc.) Imagine you are seeing or hearing these additional signals as you read the words and phrases below.

Labelling
You kids . . .
People like you . . .
Teenagers today . . .
You're like a brick-wall
You're a typical boy/girl
So that's how girls today dress, is it?
Your generation . . .

Amateur Psychologist
You're just lazy . . .
You just don't think . . .
You're acting just like a baby . . .
The trouble with you is that . . .
You're not feeling . . . you're just . . .
That's not what you're really saying . . .
You're just a trouble-maker
You're incapable of sitting still for one minute
You're not cut-out for something like that
I know you . . .
You want attention

You just don't try . . .
They don't really know you like I do
You'll never manage that
What's she's trying to say is . . .

Distancing
Children should be seen and not heard
I give up
I'm not listening

Comparisons
Your sister always did . . .
John would never treat his mother like that
Those poor little children in . . .
In my day . . .
When I was a child I . . .
Penny's a brilliant swimmer and she's only . . .
Who do you think you are?
I saw Tony the other day, he looked so grown-up. Why don't you . . .?
You're just like me, we always . . .
You and your father are like peas in a pod

Exaggerating
You always . . .
You never . . .
Can't you do anything right?
I don't seem to have taught you anything
All you want to do is sleep/play/eat
You have no respect for anything
All you ever do is complain
Everything goes in one ear and out of the other

Using age as a taunt
When you grow up . . .
That's just like a baby
Anyone would think you were a toddler
How old are you?

You're only . . .
You may think being a teenager is grown-up but . . .

Patronizing
That's so cute
That's quite good for your age
Well I suppose at least you've tried your best
Considering it's your first go . . .

Sarcasm
Were you born in a barn?
That's what you call clever, is it?
They're called shoes, are they?

Guilt-inducing
You'll be the death of me
You're giving me a headache
Children are so expensive these days.
She doesn't know she's born having only one!
Your mother's got enough on without you . . .!
Your father's done his best, you just haven't . . .
Look what you've made me do . . .
What are you trying to do to me?
See these grey hairs . . .

Prophecizing
You'll grow up to be . . .
You'll never make a . . .
One day you'll be sorry . . .
People will learn the truth about you one day
The way you're carrying on you'll become . . .

Language that can boost self-esteem

Here are some examples of the kinds of phrases which we need
to *say out loud* frequently to our children. Needless to say they
will have much more impact if they are reinforced with a loving
tone, warm smiles, appreciative hugs, exciting eyes or even
screams of joy!

Sharing positive feeling

I love you
I love being with you
I am enjoying playing with you
I love reading to you
I care so much about you
You have given me so much joy
I get such a kick out of spending the day with you
I felt so happy when I saw you doing . . .
I was so moved when you . . .
I felt so appreciated by you when you . . .
I felt so proud of you when I read . . .
I felt so excited to be seeing you again . . .

Specifying appreciation

I like the way you . . .
I like you because . . .
You are very important to me because . . .
You have a special talent for . . .
There is no one else quite like you in the whole world because . . .
You have a wonderful smile
You sing with such feeling!
You're such fun to be with because . . .
You're so creative! Just look at the way you . . .
You were witty without being hurtful
Congratulations on the way you . . .
You're a really good friend – look at the way you . . .
Sarah told me last week how good you were when . . .
Gran said she would love to have you because you always . . .
I could see that the audience were captivated when you . . .
You look great. You have such good sense of colour and . . .
Thank you for . . .
You deserve it because . . .
I admired the way you . . .

Recognition of effort and achievement

You really worked hard on that

I could see that you were trying
I know that you are doing your best
That's an amazing achievement – well done! You have . . .
Since last week, I have noticed a vast improvement . . .
Look at the progress you have made, in spite of . . .
Your talent really showed when you . . .
You can feel proud of yourself because . . .

Conveying unconditional acceptance

I accept that you are cross with me for . . .
I know that you get in bad moods sometimes but . . .
I can understand that you feel jealous . . .
It's OK for you to make mistakes
You don't have to be perfect all the time
I know that you can be aggressive but I also know that
you . . .
You have been behaving selfishly lately but I know that . . .
There are times when I get mad with you but I still love you
because . . .

Confirming trust

I trust you to . . .
I have every faith in you
I know you can do it
You're a winner!
You'll work it out, if anyone can
I can always count on you
I know that you'll cope
I am relying on you
I'd like to ask your opinion
I really value your judgement
I'd like you to help me with . . .
What do you think?
I know you are going to have a great life
I feel sure you will make a real contribution to the world

EXERCISE: **Building self-esteem**

- Using the above section as a check-list, list *three* ways in which you have built up your children's confidence during the last week.
- Now, being scrupulously honest with yourself, list three ways in which you may have knocked their self-esteem during the last month. Alternatively (or as well, if you are a glutton for punishment!) list three opportunities you may have missed to teach your child about self-love.
- Note down some goals for yourself with regard to improving your children's ability to love themselves. For example:
  - ask them to help me more often
  - ask my partner to check my language for put-downs and specific appreciations
  - set aside two hours per week for 'quality time'

'Self-esteem is a powerful human need. It is a basic human need that makes an essential contribution to the life process; it is indispensible to normal and healthy development; it has survival value.'

Dr Nathaniel Branden

Chapter 6

How to help your children develop good self-knowledge

'Our lack of self-confidence mostly comes from trying to be someone we aren't. No wonder we do not feel confident when we are living a lie. People who are cocky don't know what they have to offer.'

Anne Wilson Schaef

Self-knowledge is an all-important key to inner confidence because we cannot:

- build on and fortify ourselves with our strengths, unless we are aware of their existence in the first place
- prevent our weaknesses from sabotaging our attempts to be successful and happy, unless we know what they are to begin with

Without sound self-knowledge children tend to develop a kind of 'false-self' created from a random collection of attitudes and behaviours which they adopt and adapt in the course of trying to please the adults around them or get what they need from the world. In the process of doing this, they may abandon their instinctive interest in self-discovery and also lose that ability to relax and just 'be themselves' which we know is so vital for self-confidence.

So let's look at some practical ways in which we can help our children develop this important quality of inner confidence.

Get to know your child yourself

'My father always said he was doing this or that because he cared for me, but how could he have loved me, he didn't know me.'
Participant on Confidence Building course

Once again the above comment is not uncommonly given by people I know who lack confidence. Taking an interest in who our child really is (and not perhaps who we would like to think she is!) is not only an important way of showing a child that we care about her but is also the most important way of sparking off her interest in getting to know herself. Partly because of their feelings of closeness, many parents in my experience take their knowledge of their children too much for granted, often wrongly assuming they are carbon copies of themselves. Often it isn't until the children reach adolescence and have more and greater skills with which to assert their true personality that some parents actually meet their 'real' children. And, of course, sometimes if a child's confidence is very damaged, her true self may not *ever* materialize.

One useful way of helping children to reveal themselves to you is to ask them *open questions*. These kinds of questions are those which invite the other person to answer more than a brief 'Yes' or 'No'. The examples below illustrate what I mean by questions that can stimulate your children to reflect more on their own personality and their potential.

'I keep six honest serving men/They taught me all I knew:/ Their names are What and Why and When/And How and Where and Who.'
Rudyard Kipling

- *'Which* one do *you* like best/least? (Rather than the closed question 'Do you like this one?')
- *'What* do *you* think about . . .?' (Rather than 'That was interesting, wasn't it?)

- *'How* did *you* feel when . . .?' (Rather than 'You must have felt really frightened, is that right?')
- *'What* did *you* enjoy about . . .?' (Rather than 'Did you enjoy that?')
- *'When* do *you* find yourself getting mad or irritated?' (Rather than 'Don't you get mad when . . .?')

Discuss, challenge, listen and argue

You can help your children to formulate their individual beliefs and opinions by taking the time and effort to discuss these with them. When they are very young the subjects will obviously need to hold a personal interest for them (e.g. their favourite TV programme or what went on at school today) but as they get older you can widen the discussion to more abstract ideas or global issues.

Family arguments may not always seem the most pleasant way of spending an evening, but if they are conducted in an atmosphere of mutual respect (and not merely used as a tool for control or a release of tension) they have many invaluable uses as confidence-building tools. One of these most certainly is that arguments help children discover what is close to their hearts and what is of interest to them.

If you feel you never genuinely have anything to argue about with your children because you are so alike in your opinions and values, try to make a conscious effort to take on the 'Devil's Advocate' role occasionally just to give them a chance at least to hear themselves airing their views (and of course to practise their debating skills, which are so important for outer confidence).

Encourage risk-taking which will test their potential

I am not suggesting that you should risk the lives or limbs of your children, but certainly it will help their self-discovery if they are encouraged to do things which are not necessarily the easiest or most familiar options. In facing such challenges they may find out that they have personal strengths, interests and talents which they would never have discovered if they had always made safe choices.

Remember that in order to do this we as parents may need to devote more *time* to help our children prepare for, and handle, these new experiences, especially if they need guidance on how to handle their fear and worry of doing something wrong or failing. Very few children's confidence is actually improved by being 'thrown in at the deep end' without preparation and support. (See Chapter 11 for guidance on how to help your child handle fear.)

For those of you with a tendency to be over-protective either because of your own negative experiences or because we have a particularly 'fragile' child, you will need to take special care not to sabotage your children's risk-taking with discouraging comments. As the latter usually come wrapped up in the guise of 'convincing, caring advice' you may need to ask someone close to you to monitor your language; you may even need to keep your distance from your children while they are trying out risks for themselves. (Thank goodness for resources like the Guides, Scouts and Outward Bound centres, which offer adventurous children a safe haven from fearful, over-protective parents!)

Give specific compliments and positive feedback

Every parent knows how important it is for a child's self-esteem to give him compliments and I am sure you will already be doing this, but could you improve the way you give your positive feedback so that it will help your children get to know more about himself and his particular strengths? Here are some examples you can use to check your general style – please note that there is nothing very wrong about using the phrases given in brackets, it's just that *sometimes* it's a good idea to make a special effort to give more specific compliments.

- 'I really like that picture . . . you seem to have a good eye for colour and detail.' (Rather than 'What a lovely picture, I wish I could draw as well as that.')
- 'I felt so proud of you when I heard you singing on stage because you have a very special talent for getting the audience's attention.' (Rather than 'You were great . . . everyone loved you.')
- 'You look so pretty in that dress because blue seems to bring out the colour in your lovely eyes.' (Rather than 'You look pretty today.')
- 'Well done, this is an excellent report. I was especially

interested to note that you again did very well in . . . and
. . . It seems that you have a real talent in those subjects,
what do you think?' (Rather than 'That's brilliant – you are
clever.')

Give direct, honest and specific criticism

Many parents are so terrified of knocking their children's
confidence that they hold back too much on giving criticism.
Given in the right way, criticism is an *essential* tool for improving
self-knowledge. Children are more likely to listen and absorb
your negative feedback if it is given in an assertive, constructive
way. Here are some guidelines you can use as a checklist.

Do –

– whenever possible choose an **appropriate time and place**
(e.g. not just before bed when your child is tired, or in
front of friends, or first thing in the morning). Most
criticism can be postponed for a discussion at a later time
in a private place, or a more relaxed time (though of course
with very young children it is best not to delay too long)
– start, if possible, with a positive comment or observation
(e.g. 'I love you very much, Johnny, but when you . . .' or
'Generally, I think that you work very hard at your
homework, but last week . . .')
– indicate that you have some **empathy** with their difficulty
or feeling (e.g. 'It must be difficult being the youngest
sometimes, but . . .' or 'When I was at school, I used to
feel frustrated as well, so I think I know how you feel
but . . .')
– avoid language which will deflate their self-esteem (see
Chapter 5, pages 89–91)
– focus on **behaviour** rather than personality ('You're eating
very messily' rather than 'You're a mucky thing'!)
– as with giving compliments, be **specific** and not too general

('I get irritated when you leave your books and shoes in the hall' rather than 'Your untidiness drives me mad')

- stick to **one** criticism at a time whenever possible (Resist 'while we're at it, last week . . . and there's another thing . . .')

- encourage your children to **respond** particularly with **self-evaluation**, but make sure that you give them time to express themselves because they are very unlikely to be able to match your articulacy. (' . . . that's my feeling, but what do *you* think of your report – do you think you need to improve your concentration?')

- stick to **your own feelings and reactions**, unless you have a very good reason for including the opinion of any others who cannot speak for themselves (avoid 'I'm sure Grandma would be shocked if she'd seen you . . .' or 'I don't know what your headmaster would have to say if I told him . . .')

Encourage awareness of feeling

The way individual children handle their feelings is in part determined by their genes; some will let their feelings 'all hang out' and others will be less expressive. Whatever a child's style of expressing feelings, it is important for inner confidence to have an *awareness* of emotions. (This knowledge is an essential foundation for teaching children the skills of managing their emotions in an assertive and appropriate manner, which we will be looking at in Chapter 11).

One of the best ways of getting children to become more aware of their feelings is **first to disclose and share your own** before asking them about theirs (e.g. 'I'm fed up because it's raining again today. Are you a bit disappointed too or don't you mind?').

Another good way is to share your observations of their non-verbal behaviour, being careful not to interpret too much for them. ('Your voice doesn't sound very excited to me. Are you really feeling pleased about it?' or 'You seemed to be scowling at Michael, are you cross with him about something or have I got it wrong?').

Use drama, art and games to increase self-awareness

With most young children, these kinds of methods present the easiest way for them to explore their values, and feelings, and to experiment with their strengths and their weaknesses. There are now lots of games on the market which families can play together that will help you to help your children become more self-aware. Simple drama methods are even cheaper and may suit some children better. For example, most children love to play 'let's pretend I am you and you are me.' These kind of impersonation games come very naturally to most children and they are often uncomfortably (for parents) skilled at them! Together with gentle teasing, these games can be a very powerful way of helping all the members of a family to own and accept their particular idiosyncrasies and weaknesses!

Alternatively, if your child shows an inclination for self-expression through art, you could use this medium to initiate discussion about feelings, and thoughts. Beware, however, of getting over-enthusiastic in the role of amateur art therapist, and always remember that you are a parent and not a clinical professional being paid to give an objective assessment. (I know only too well from my own experience how the role of parent and therapist rarely mesh co-operatively together, and your children will most certainly prefer the former!)

Teach self-evaluation

Encourage your children to assess regularly their own behaviour and performance. Self-evaluation is now widely used in schools, so older children will benefit from having extra practice in this skill. Make an effort to hold on to your own judgements until after you have encouraged your children to express theirs. For example, if your child shows you two pictures, one of which you are sure denotes genius, hold on to your bubbling admiration until you have asked which one he or she prefers and why. Or, choosing a time when you are feeling particularly patient, if your children are pulling out each other's hair, hold on to your horror, separate them and when they have calmed down ask them what *they* think of their behaviour.

EXERCISE: **Helping my children to get to know themselves**

- In whatever language is appropriate for your children, make a point this week of asking them what they consider to be their greatest strengths and their best achievements. Does their evaluation match your own? If not, note down what you can do to try to get to know your children better or how you can improve their self-knowledge, if you think they have an unrealistic picture of their personality and potential. (Obviously you will be making an allowance for some grandiosity appropriate to their years!)
- Write down three open questions you could ask your children in the next week.
- Write down three examples of criticisms you regularly make of your children, and use the guidelines listed above to check that you are expressing them effectively.

Chapter 7

Helping your children to set goals

I must confess to having some mixed feelings about goal-setting for children. My 'inner child' (which still craves more space for the spontaneity and freedom that were curtailed in my early years) resents the idea of structuring children, and 'argues' that this can kill their creativity and set limits on their potential. The sensible 'adult' part of me counters this argument with the knowledge that goals give a sense of purpose to life and also increase children's sense of security.

Goal-setting's positive features always win this argument. I know that if we have goals (at whatever age) we feel that we have some personal control over the world around us and our destiny. And even though a child's goals may look minuscule set beside our own grand life-plans, they are equally important for the growth of his or her confidence. After all, a seven-year-old's goal of trying to swim three widths of the pool before the end of term can be as (if not more) challenging and motivating than the financial executive's objective to recoup an investment within three years. But, when we are encouraging our children to set goals for themselves, there are a number of points it is helpful to bear in mind if we want their confidence to be enhanced while they are reaching for their stars. Once again, you can use what follows as a checklist.

Children's goals and targets

When helping your children establish goals, remember that they need to be:

- **Personal** – and always set with the *individual* child's potential in mind. This may mean, therefore, that the goals of eight children, even of the same age and background, may have to vary enormously. We need to encourage our children to concentrate their minds on going for what they want or need rather than looking constantly over their shoulders at the targets of others around them. And, perhaps even more importantly, we need to restrain ourselves from making comparisons. This isn't to say that very *general* achievement guidelines cannot be useful, of course they can. After all, our children have to live in a world which will judge them by prevailing standards of society, and they will have to accept this however unfair it may seem at times. But, with regard to confidence-building, it is vital that we emphasize that *personal* goals have as much, if not more value than those that are set by others in the world around them.
- **Realistic** – and down to earth. Children need to know that, although they have vast potential resources within their minds and bodies, each of us does have limitations. Encouraging children to set themselves goals that are too challenging for them can have a very depressing effect on the growth of their confidence. I know that many people sincerely believe that – with the power of pure, unadulterated positive thinking – only the sky need be the limit. They would argue that it is therefore important not to deflate but rather to encourage children's natural grandiosity. But the building of a sound and *lasting* inner confidence needs a more pragmatic approach – at least most of the time. (All of us can benefit sometimes from the temporary spurt of energy that this kind of 'magical' belief in all things possible can give.)
- **Graduated** – and broken down into very small manageable

steps. The most secure kind of confidence is that which is built on a *continual* stream of achievements, each of which takes children nearer and nearer their main goal. Ideally each step needs to be just slightly more difficult than the last, so that the chances of success are very high and there needs to be as short a time-gap between each step as can be reasonably managed, so that the energy generated by the feeling of success can be channelled into the next stage.

Some children will, of course, be very impatient (especially at the start of their step-by-step 'programme'). Others will find that, as they get going, they may be able to move at a faster pace than originally planned but, especially in the early stages, try not to let them get too carried away with their success and be tempted to skip too many steps. Even though they could reach their end goal a little more quickly, they may lose out on gaining the psychological strength which comes with the steady drip-feed of small successes.

- **Rewarded** – as *soon* as possible after *each* step has been taken. The psychological jargon to describe this kind of reward is *'positive reinforcement'*; it is probably the most powerful motivational tool and aid to learning and success that your child will ever have. These rewards do not have to break your bank or ruin your children's teeth. In fact, the simple but regular treats such as extra time to play, a big hug from you or stars on a wall chart are generally much more effective than far-off dreams of mountain bikes or red Ferraris! As your children grow, you can encourage them to set and administer their own rewards, because self-reinforcement works even greater wonders for our confidence!

- **Flexible** – partly because they develop at such a rapid pace, children's goal-posts may have to move around much more quickly than ours. So check that old messages about 'sticking to it', which may surface from your auto-parent, do not interfere with your children's need (and right) to change their minds frequently. What is important is to

check that they are not just abandoning one set of goals but are working towards *replacing* them with another set which may be more challenging and exciting and, therefore, more ultimately rewarding – even though they may first need to have a period of restful and creative aimlessness.

- **Respected** – however petty, strange or alien they may seem to us. This may seem an obvious point to caring parents who would never consciously put down their children's aims and ambitions, but even the most caring among us sometimes does just this without realizing it. We may find ourselves overly teasing a child about an 'obsession' with a particular interest; giving more attention to the goals we can relate to have an investment in seeing completed; or simply not noticing the small steps of a child's successes.

EXERCISE: **My children's goals**

- List a number of goals which your children have at the

moment and check each of them against the list of
guidelines above.

• Make a conscious effort to talk to your children
individually over the next month or so about their current
'dreams' for the future, and see if you or they can make
any connection between their present goals and targets. If
this is possible (and let's hope it is!), see if together you
can work out a series of progressive steps which could lead
from one to the other. With young children this exercise
will probably take the form of a casual 'day-dreaming' chat,
but with older children it could translate into a more
structured life-plan. Either style would give anyone's inner
confidence a bit of a boost!

'We are what and where we are because we have first imagined it.'
Donald Curtis

Chapter 8

Helping your children to think positively

Negative thinking is not natural – it is simply a bad habit. Nevertheless it is a habit which many children begin to pick up from the world around them at a very early age. Like all bad habits, it is much easier to eradicate if it is 'nipped in the bud' at an early stage.

Negative thinking has become so embedded in our Western culture that it is now taking a whole personal development industry to help adults beat the disease. Even though I earn part of my bread and butter writing books and running courses on how to kick this destructive habit, I know that I would much prefer to live in a society where children's *natural* positive outlook on themselves and their lives was not so routinely contaminated by despair and cynicism.

I have no doubt that negative thinking also corrodes self-confidence. You must know yourself that when you are in a good mood and *expecting* things to go well, you both feel and appear more self-assured – and, very importantly, are likely to be much more successful at whatever you are trying to do. It's no wonder that shrewd employers, with a good eye for profit, include in their selection procedures questions designed to reveal whether applicants for jobs are happy and positive as well as qualified and able.

Of course the most powerful way of helping your child to remain a positive thinker (yes, we were all born that way inclined!) is to be one yourself, but even if you are, children will pick up negative habits from other sources such as friends, TV, books and even their teachers at school. Here are some tips on how to counteract these unwanted depressing influences.

Ways to help your children think positively

Mornings

Help them start the day with positive thoughts and impressions. This does not mean that you necessarily have to be extremely bright and cheery at 7 a.m. every day, but you can make an effort not to be the opposite! For example, you can try to:

- Make an extra effort to get up a little earlier so that there is time for gentle chat about what everyone is looking forward to that day.
- Discourage the sharing of moans and miseries, saying that they can be discussed later in the day.
- Make sure that your children's minds aren't being fed with a depressing negative input about problems which they have absolutely no power to influence or control. (If you yourself are addicted to an early morning dose of bulletins on war, famine, political disappointments or traffic chaos, why not try headphones?)

Bedtime

Help them end the day on a positive note – most parents will do this almost automatically for babies and very young children but often let the habit slip as they get older. You could check that you haven't lost the 'lullaby habit' by asking yourself these kinds of questions:

- Do we give the children a quiet time in the evening to share good impressions and achievements of the day and reflect on what we are all looking forward to tomorrow?
- Is the content of the book or programme they are reading or watching giving a positive view of the world, or is it unnecessarily frighteninig or gloomy? (If it is, you may of course want to suggest another book or programme, or at least 'counter' the negativity with some positive reassurance.)

Self-talk

Discourage your children from talking to themselves in a negative way. Instead, try to encourage them regularly to use positive affirmations to give themselves a boost and replace obsessive worrying thoughts. For example:

'I can do it.'
'I'm a great footballer.'
'I'm confident and in control.'
'I like the way I look.'
'Exams are a challenge – I enjoy challenges and find them exciting.'

Generalizations

Help them to rephrase what they have said with more specific rational and correct statements, while still allowing them space to vent their negative feeling. For example:

'Girls are awful'	'Some girls really annoy me.'
'Buses are always late.'	'This bus has been late twice this week.'
'Exam questions never have anything to do with the syllabus.'	'Some exam questions don't cover subjects we have studied.'

Exaggerations

Help your children to be aware of when they are using exaggerations in a depressing way, replace them with a more correct statement. For example:

'I never get anything right.'   'I've done it wrong again.'
'The teacher never listens to   'Sometimes when I ask a
me.'   question the teacher ignores
                                 me.'

'He always ruins the game.'   'He's spoilt this game.'

Exclusions

Help them to see when they are ignoring the positive aspects of a situation and seeing only the negative side of the story or the facts. But don't forget to empathize with their feelings or the difficult aspects of what they may be trying to achieve. For example:

Your child says:
   'It's boring at Grandma's – there's no one to play with.'
You can say:
   'I know it's difficult because you haven't got your friends there, but aren't you forgetting that you like going to her park and she lets you stay up to watch videos?' (Instead of, for example: 'You always moan about going, but you enjoy it when you get there.')
Your child says:
   'I hate school, I don't want to go back.'
You can say:
   'I know there's lots of things you don't like about school and you get very frustrated, but you do enjoy seeing your friends and you do really like Maths and Science.' (Instead of: 'I know you. Of course you really don't hate school – just remember they are the best days of your life and they'll soon be over!')

Predictions

Point out when your child's predictions are unnecessarily and unfairly negative, and if possible suggest replacing with the reality and hope of a more positive outcome. Remember that your job is not to counter their gloom with a *false* prediction or unreasonable hope, but to teach them not to undermine their confidence with self-defeating talk. Once again, be careful not to dismiss their feelings and try starting with a statement which shows that you respect them. For example:

Your child says:
  'There won't be anyone there that I'll get on with.'
You can say:
  'I can understand that you're worried that you won't make any friends, but there's going to be a lot of children to choose from and the chances are actually very high that you are going to get on with at least one of them. So, when you start to worry, why not tell yourself this is a great opportunity to meet a new friend and it will be much more likely to happen if you go in smiling!' (Instead of saying, for example: 'Don't be so gloomy, of course, you'll make friends.')

Your child says:
  'I know I am going to lose even though we are supposed to be the same standard. I never have any luck with her – I haven't won one game against her yet.'
You can say:
  'Yes, I can see that you're anxious about this one, but the fact that you have lost before does not mean you'll lose today. Instead of worrying, why not tell yourself this is going to be a great game and your first win?' (Instead of: 'Don't be silly – of course you'll win.')

Your child says:
  'I can't decide because whatever I decide will probably turn out to be wrong.'
You can say:
  'It must be worrying to have to make such a difficult choice, but the reality is that you could be making the *right* decision.

113

So why not tell yourself that it can turn out to be OK and that the very worst that can happen is that you will learn from your mistake if it does go wrong?' (Instead of: 'If you never make decisions in life, you'll never get anywhere.')

Your child says:

'What does it matter if I smoke? I'll probably get run over or the world will blow itself up before I get the chance to get cancer anyway.'

You can say:

'I know it's really hard to deprive yourself of a pleasure when you can't be certain that you're going to benefit from doing so, and the world does sometimes seem to be so unpredictable and frightening. But the reality is that you stand a good chance of surviving for very many years, and you have very many exciting plans for your life. So why not tell yourself that life looks as though it's going to be great and you're going to be there to enjoy it?' (Instead of: 'Well if you're going to take that attitude, you might as well give up now, there's no point in doing anything towards your future if you don't think positively.')

EXERCISE: **Encouraging positive thinking**

• Using the above examples to guide you, practise your ability to turn negative thinking into a more positive approach by rephrasing the following and including an expression of empathy for your child's feelings:

1. 'I'll never be able to do this.'
2. 'Jan always beats me, it's not worth trying.'
3. 'It's bound to rain and spoil it all.'
4. 'There's no point in telling her, she won't listen.'
5. 'He won't want to play.'
6. 'I'll probably fail anyway.'
7. 'I'm sure I'll never get in, they only accept 50 per cent of all applicants.'
8. 'It'll be just my luck, I'll go all the way there and no one will be in.'

9. 'What's the point of studying all these years when there probably won't be any jobs at the end of it?'
10. 'You wouldn't understand.'

- Over the next week make a special effort to look out for examples of negative thinking and try either to rephrase them in your head or directly with the person concerned (especially if he or she happens to be one of your children or your partner!)

'There's no sadder sight than a young pessimist.'

Mark Twain

Part 3

Improving your child's outer confidence

In this section we will be working on ways in which you can help your children acquire the following four main qualities of outer confidence:

- Good Communication
- Self-presentation
- Assertiveness
- Emotional Control

Each of these qualities is essential if you want your children to be able to make full use of their inner confidence – unless, of course they are destined for a life on a desert island!

Unlike the qualities of inner confidence, which are in the main acquired through children's experience of their relationships with you and the other significant people in their early childhood, many of the above qualities are ones they will be taught outside the home, ʳarticularly at school, and by oher major channels of social learning such as the media. Indeed, many countries are now investing large amounts of money in training teachers and youth leaders to teach these outer confidence skills, and also subsidizing some attempts in the media to help children in this way. So you may find that your child is having lessons in Listening, Giving Presentations, Coping with Criticism, etc. alongside Maths, Physics and French.

However good our children's school or TV programmes, as parents we can still make an enormous contribution just by integrating some of the learning of these outer confidence skills into our everyday interactions and constantly encouraging and monitoring our children's progress.

Please remember that the material in the following chapters is not intended to be used for 'formal' teaching sessions with your children, which would be both inappropriate and counter-productive. Rather I am intending that it be used to raise your awareness of children's needs in this area, and to give you some ideas of what kind of help children who are experiencing difficulties may benefit from.

Chapter 9

Communication skills and self-presentation

Good communication skills are essential 'tools of the trade' for confident people. Unfortunately, however, they are not provided free of charge at birth, they have to be *learned*. In this chapter we will be looking at ways in which we can actively help our children develop some of the major communication skills. Maybe many

of you, like me, did not yourselves acquire these skills in the course of your own childhood. If this should be so, why not try them out first? As I have already said many times in this book, your influence as a role-model has more power than anything you can directly say or do with your children.

Conversation

Most young children are chatterboxes and love to strike up conversations with everybody they meet. In fact, if there's no one around they'll talk with the dog, a teddy or an imaginary friend. But as they grow up many of these natural conversationalists, even if they have good self-esteem, will develop such a fear of talking with others that they become very isolated and lonely. So what goes wrong?

Quite often the reason is that these children never learn to progress beyond 'toddler conversation', which actually consists of talking 'at' others, almost irrespective of whether the other person is listening. As a result, they will have found fewer and fewer people wanting to engage in conversation with them and so they lose their natural inclination to start chatting. If your child appears to develop this kind of problem, you can help by:

- **giving them practice** by chatting to them regularly from a very early age and giving them an opportunity to meet with a wide range of people who will also be willing to talk to them (avoiding those who still think children should be seen and not heard!)
- **improving their listening skills.** You can do this by asking them not to interrupt you but to listen carefully instead. When you have finished talking then ask them to repeat what you have just said, or to tell you in their own words what they think you have just said. When they are older you can encourage them to do this, without being asked, with other people. In doing this you will have taught them a very important skill, which is called by psychologists *reflective listening*. This particular technique is now taught each week to thousands and

thousands of caring and ambitious professional adults who are willing to pay large sums of money to learn it because they know how much it will improve their relationships and ability to communicate.

- **insisting on manners** such as not talking with a full mouth or while chewing gum or rudely interrupting or any other behaviour which generally offends people and tends to curtail conversations
- **explaining cultural differences** and demonstrating how we have to adapt our conversational style to suit different people and different situations
- **valuing small talk** and not dismissing it as worthless because it is superficial. (I am continually asked by adults who have never learned this skill to include small-talk practice in my confidence courses.) As your children begin to initiate friendships, you can explain the value of small talk in helping us to relax and get to know a wide range of people, while protecting conversations from getting too personal or too 'heavy' before the relationship is ready for it. If you have teenagers who are finding the 'chatting-up' game hard to start, help them to identify the kinds of subjects *they* can use as low-risk conversation openers (e.g. the number of people present, the weather, a current sporting event, the music, etc.).
- **making them aware of non-verbal language** and teaching them that it has more impact on listeners than the words which we use. Help them to be conscious of their own body language and to notice that of other people.
- **helping them to judge when humour is appropriate** and inappropriate by giving them honest feedback on how they use it
- **talking to them about self-disclosure** and letting them know that this is one of the best ways to get other people to open up and become closer and more intimate. (Again, this news may be of particular interest to teenagers!) But make sure they also know the dangers of getting into 'heavy' conversations too quickly.

Debate

How good are your children at arguing? I am sure many of you may answer – 'too good!' Your experience may tell you that this is a skill which your children practise all too often and the last thing on your mind is to look at ways which will encourage them to use it more frequently and skillfully!

I can empathize with you – I have a very argumentative family and there have been many occasions when I have wished for more peace and harmony in my home! But when I am in a stronger and more adult frame of mind, I thoroughly enjoy the stimulating atmosphere of debate and discussion and feel particularly proud of both my daughters' undoubted skills in this area. I also know that these skills have been, and will continue to be, invaluable aids to their confidence and will certainly help them achieve their dreams and ambitions.

So, *sometimes*, instead of using your energy (often pointlessly) to find ways to stop your children from arguing, why not use it to help them to argue more skilfully and constructively? (Be careful not to sound patronizing.) You can do this by:

- **developing their articulacy** by helping them to say what you think they really mean when they appear to be 'getting their wires crossed' or in danger of going silent or running away because they cannot express themselves
- **improving their ability to put their point across** in as concise a form as possible by highlighting their unnecessary examples or arguments
- **letting them know when others appear to be 'switching off'** because perhaps they are 'holding forth' too long or being too pernickety
- **stopping them from using aggressive techniques and personal attacks** which are hurting others and perhaps forcing them into an unnecessary defensive attack, instead of listening to the argument
- **encouraging them to stand up for their right to an explanation** when it is obvious that they have not understood what the other person had said

- **pointing out when they have made assumptions** about the other person's knowledge or feelings
- **helping them to realize when their emotions and not their heads have taken control**
- **insisting that each party has an equal and fair chance to be heard**
- **pointing out when they have moved the goal-posts** and the debate has gone down a new track
- **helping them end the debate** by agreeing a time limit to the discussion or argument and encouraging them, whenever possible, to finish on a positive or amicable note (e.g. 'Well, we've given that subject a good airing, and at least we are all clear about what each of us thinks' or 'Let's, for the moment, agree to disagree.')
- **complimenting them** when they have debated well, even when they have won an argument against you!

Public speaking

This is another area in which very young children have few inhibitions. If a nursery school teacher asks for a volunteer to read or talk in front of the class, he or she is usually inundated with eager would-be performers. But if a colleague should ask the same question 10 years later, how many offers do you think there would be? By the time most children reach their teenage years, not only have they usually lost their enthusiasm for speaking in public but it is very likely they will also be quite inept at practising the art. What often happens is that a select few (usually the more extrovert or aggressive ones) soon become the 'voice' of any group they are part of. As a result their public speaking skills have ample opportunity to grow and develop. All the others, who may have the potential to be much more charismatic and articulate, are left far behind, hoping and praying that no one will notice them.

This is why it is important that we, as parents, keep an eye on what is happening to our children in this area of their development. Today, with so much emphasis on oral work and examination in schools, even if you feel your children are destined for a 'quiet life', it is essential that, at the very least, they have the skills to communicate their ideas and knowledge in small groups – otherwise they will most certainly underachieve.

Unless your children have very great difficulties in this area, if you help them to observe and respect the three golden rules below they will invariably reach a good-enough standard.

The three golden 'Ps' of public speaking

Whether your children (or you!) are addressing three or three hundred people, they will do so with increased confidence and skill if they take care to be:

● Practised ● Prepared ● Positive ●

Practised

Emphasize to your children that being practised is the major key to putting a point of view across publicly. Let them know that, unless there is a very good physical reason which limits them, *anyone* can *learn* the art, even though not everyone will enjoy practising it to the same extent.

And for you, there are two main points to remember about practice:

a) the more fun it is, the more your children will learn and
b) the sooner you start, the easier it will be for you and
   them.

So, even if *your* children are still toddlers, they can begin, for example, by putting on 'plays' or shows for you at home or participating in certain kinds of games (e.g. 'Let's pretend we're on TV or we have a market stall'.) And, although I appreciate that these kinds of activities will initially demand more of your energy and time, they are an investment in your child's personal development and ones which will benefit not only your child but you in the future. So, when the call of the video feels more tempting, just remind yourself how much less stressful and more rewarding it will be to parent a confident child for the rest of your life!

As your children get older, if they still need extra help you can, of course, encourage them to join drama clubs or other groups which will give them opportunities to speak up in front of others. If such activities do not appeal, you can still do much to help at home. You could, for example, listen to them rehearsing presentations for school or, as they gain in confidence, you could record them on a cassette or a video. (Recorders for the latter can now be hired very reasonably for a day, the cost could even be shared between several families.)

Preparation

Make sure that your children do not fall for the myth that only the people who speak brilliantly 'off the cuff' are the truly confident presenters. The vast majority of confident people take great care to 'think before speaking', and they always do as much preparation as they can for any presentation or performance. So, encourage your children from an early age to do similarly rather than relying on the capricous charms of the 'gift of the gab'.

On your part it is important not to assume that your children's teacher or instructor is able to help them prepare adequately. Whether they may be talking to the class about their summer holiday or giving a presentation on an academic research project, you could, for example, set aside some time to encourage them (and teach them, if necessary) how to:

a) think seriously and creatively about their subject
b) consider the needs and interests of their 'audience'
c) make very clear concise and easy-to-read notes or visual aids

Positive

During their school life (and later in their adult life!) your children will, no doubt, be called upon to talk publicly on all sorts of subjects that they consider boring (and are convinced others do as well!). Why not suggest that they use these opportunities to practise their skills at giving *positive* presentations, so that when they are talking about something interesting they will do it even more confidently and expertly? Emphasize, by pointing out good examples on TV, how much easier and more interesting it is to listen to speakers who:

a) smile and look relaxed
b) use a strong, lively tone of voice
c) indicate either through their words or eye contact that they have noticed their audience and are enjoying talking to them
d) start and finish on a positive note (rather than using the familiar self-put-downs such as 'I don't want to bore you for long' or 'I expect you have had enough of my voice by now.')

Self-presentation

Now we are entering a minefield! Disagreements between generations in the area of self-presentation must be as inevitable as dawn following dusk, so you may want to keep the kid-gloves handy as you work through this chapter!

Before discussing this issue any further, perhaps I ought make clear what I mean by self-presentation. I use this term to cover the range of ways in which we say, consciously or unconsciously, to both ourselves and the world, 'This is me and this is what I am about.' Primarily, children convey this message through their personal appearance.

Perhaps in an ideal, accepting, non-judgemental world, self-presentation would not be of so much concern to someone trying to help their children with confidence, but whether we like the idea or not, we all judge others very largely on appearance. This is an important lesson to teach our children. On the other hand, we also need to make them aware that they can endanger their inner confidence if they spend too much time and energy adapting their self-presentation to please and impress the world around them.

So how can we help our children to walk the delicate tightrope between the needs of their outer and inner confidence?

- **Body language** – teach them from an early age how important this is and help them to be aware of when they are using it appropriately (*and* inappropriately)
- **Experimentation and choice** – give them as much scope as possible to do this, especially when they are young. This may mean abandoning a few treasured dreams and resolutions (e.g. 'when I have children, I will never let them wear . . .') and allowing them to make their own decisions about what they wear and when they wear it (money, weather and school rules permitting!). These decisions are an important means by which children

discover and express their individual identity and values and we can and should expect this process to continue at least right through later adolescence. We should also remember that their appearance is one of the few means which children have to assert their separateness from us, and as such it will inevitably become an important symbol of independence.

- **Knowledge** – before children can choose a style of presentation, they need to have information which many adults just take for granted (for example: social conventions, relative costs, differences in quality of various materials, etc.) These may need to be explained carefully to children in terms which they can understand, so they can make *informed* decisions before being put down by adults or older brothers and sisters who may laugh at the naïveté of their choices. (Doesn't this happen all too often?)
- **Feedback** – this must be honest and constructive. We do not help our children's inner or outer confidence by giving 'blanket compliments' ('You look handsome/lovely in anything.') We also need to remember to give them specific reasons why we don't like or approve of their choices. For example:

'I think if you wear that it might not look appropriate for the occasion' (rather than 'Are you mad? You can't go there looking like that.') or,

'If your handwriting was neater, the teacher would find it easier to read' (rather than 'I don't know what the teacher is going to make of such messy work.')

EXERCISE: **Improving communication and presentation**

- Using the check-lists above to help you, note down one practical piece of action you can take to help your child during the next month to become more skilled and confident in his or her ability to:

  - make conversation
  - enter into debate

— speak up in front of a group

- Note down some helpful feedback you could give your child on self-presentation (perhaps a specific compliment to share), or something practical you could do to help him or her to be more aware or interested in self-presentation (e.g. a rummage through your wardrobes together; a relaxed shopping trip; a book on colour coordination from the library for you to read together).
- Over the next few weeks take notice of your child's use of body language, checking that it is being used appropriately. If it is not, think what you could do to help (e.g. use watching a TV programne together and pointing out the body language or showing them the cartoon below, etc.).

'It's only shallow people who do not judge by appearances.'

Oscar Wilde

Chapter 10
Assertiveness

Learning how to be assertive helps us to be ourselves, to respect our own human rights and also to go directly, and energetically, for what we really want without trampling on the needs and rights of others.

If you can integrate some basic assertiveness training into your children's everyday lives, your efforts will not only strengthen their confidence, but also make them much easier to live with!

Although the word 'assertive' has in the last few years become very freely used, it is still frequently confused with styles of behaviour that are more aggressive, or even passive. While all three basic styles have their uses and misuses, it is the assertive one which is most often used by confident people and is the one you should encourage your children to adopt as their basic 'operating mode'.

If as you are reading this you are realizing that you are not very clear what 'being assertive' is all about, maybe the following summary will help to clarify the differences between the three basic styles of attitude and behaviour.

Aggressive, passive and assertive styles

Aggressive

Basic attitude: 'The world is a tough place, but I am the most important person in it and I am prepared to hurt anyone or anything that gets in the way of my happiness or success.'

Typical behaviour: domineering, selfish, forceful, attacking, insensitive, hurtful, righteous, bombastic, prejudiced, blaming, punitive and mistrustful.

Passive

Basic attitude: 'The world is a scary and difficult place to be in and other people are more important and better than me, so I have to please, or appear to please them.'

Typical behaviour: meek, aquiescent, compliant, submissive, resigned, docile, helpless; self-blaming; self-effacing; long-suffering; manipulative.

Assertive

Basic attitude: 'The world is an OK place and I am just as important as anyone else in it and, like everyone else, I have a right to success and happiness.'

Typical behaviour: self-respecting, fair-minded, honest, direct, expressive, challenging, upright, respectful, trusting, co-operative, persistent, innovative and decisive.

If, after reading the above table you find yourself still confused, I would strongly advise you at the very least to do some reading before trying to help your child in this area. My book *Assert Yourself* includes a short self-help programme that might be a good starting point.

If you feel your knowledge in this area is good enough, here are some ways in which you can help your children develop their assertiveness.

Teach them their rights

Before your children begin to learn how to behave assertively, they should be convinced that they have a *right* to do so. Unfortunately, they will be constantly exposed to the still prevalent cultural belief that equates 'good, nice children' with 'submissive, humble children'.

I have listed on page 133 some of the rights that you may need to emphasize to your children, because these are the ones that I find are so commonly abused or questioned. The benefit of having a list like this is that it can easily be learned and can become firmly embedded in yours and your children's mind. Each right can then be easily 'accessed' and re-stated if support or reinforcement are necessary. For example:

- if your child should tell you that he or she is too frightened to ask the teacher for an explanation, for fear of being thought to be stupid, you can say – 'Remember, it is OK not to know everything.'
- if you observe he or she is taking too long to make a decision and you suspect it is out of fear of making the wrong one, you can say 'It is OK for you to make mistakes sometimes.'

Remember that the more often you repeat these rights to your children the more likely it is that these rights will become a permanent part of their belief system. Many adults who have been on my Assertiveness Training or Confidence Building courses have made this list a permanent feature – on loo doors, kitchen cupboards or office notice-boards – because they have found it such a powerful support. If you have an imaginative child he or she may enjoy making a colourful poster of his or her personal list.

The following could be used either as it is or 'translated' into language more suitable for your own particular children. (For

My Rights

I have a right to:

- Ask for what I want
  - even though people might say 'no'
- Ask for help
  - even if people seem too busy or don't want to help
- Have ideas
  - even if people think they are silly
- Feel my feelings
  - even when people say I shouldn't have those feelings
- Make mistakes
  - especially when I have tried my very best
- Try and try again
  - even if some people may think I can't do it
- Change my mind sometimes
  - even when people think I shouldn't
- Have some secrets
  - even though some people may think I should tell them or show them everything
- Choose to be alone sometimes
  - even if everybody else is with someone
- Say 'no' sometimes
  - especially to strangers and bullies
- Complain when it's not fair
  - even though I may still have to do it, or not do it
- Be proud when I do well
  - even though some people may be upset because I did better than them

example, you might substitute 'I have a right to . . .' with 'It's OK to . . .') If you do rewrite your own list, remember to make each sentence as concise as possible so that it is easy to repeat and learn. Please feel free to edit or add to the list, according to your child's needs and your individual values. You will notice that I have included opposite each of these rights a sentence which reinforces or explains its meaning. When you write out your list you can do something similar if you think your children would find it helpful.

Teach them how to ask effectively for what they want

Sometimes children do not make their requests assertively, simply because they find it difficult to express what they actually want. So, from time to time when you observe your children asking for something in an aggressive or manipulative way, instead of just responding with a criticism (e.g. 'Don't bully him' or 'You won't get round me that way!') suggest sitting down for five minutes to talk about what it is they are trying to say. You can help them to articulate their requests in a more assertive way. Point out to them that they are more likely to get what they want (and keep their friends!) if they remember the following points:

An **assertive** request is one that is:

- **direct** and does not beat about the bush
- **concise** and doesn't use lots of unnecessary words
- **polite** and shows respect for the other person's situation or feelings (e.g. 'I know that you really like that game, but . . .') or 'I can see that you're busy Dad, but . . .'
- **positive** and indicates, if only through the tone of voice, that you expect to get what you are asking for (in contrast to 'I know you are going to get cross when I ask you . . .')
- **non-threatening** and doesn't include even a 'veiled' punishment (e.g. 'I'll be upset if you don't . . .')
- **non-manipulative** (e.g. 'John's mother always . . .')

As soon as you feel your children are old enough, you could also teach them the famous **'broken record'** technique which will help them to **persist** with their requests without getting aggressive. Point out that this method is not a 'cure-all' for disagreements but a way of putting your point across without getting aggressive in situations where you are very sure that you are in the right. Tell them that if it does not work they can assure themselves that they have tried their very best and that perhaps it is time to seek help from you or some other adult.

The broken record

Technique: calmly repeat over and over again what you want, without responding to unnecessary arguments or put-downs.

Situation: Jane urgently needs the skirt she lent her sister last week (it is the *only* thing that fits her properly!). Usually these requests end in blazing rows with neither getting what she wants. Note how effective *'broken record'* can be in this 'panic' situation, even though it may not provide all the answers to impassioned sibling rivalry!

Jane: Can I please have back the skirt which you borrowed last week?

Rachel: What do you want it back for? You never wear it.

Jane: Can I have the skirt back, please?

Rachel: You're always wanting your things, what about the leggings you took from my room?

Jane: Can I have the skirt back, please?

Rachel: Why do you always leave things to the last minute? Couldn't you have sorted out what you were going to wear last night?

Jane: Can I have the skirt back, please?

Rachel: Oh, all right, I'll get it – but you're not borrowing anything from me tonight.

Teach them that compromise is OK

There is so much encouragement in our society for children to feel competitive and to go for the all-out win that you may need to counteract these messages by explaining that confident people do not *always* have to win, they can feel equally successful if they have managed to get a compromise solution. The best way to teach them how to negotiate a compromise is to let them test their skills on you! Of course, you must make it very clear from the start when an issue is negotiable and when it is not – and, when it is, take time to listen and be willing to move your goal-posts.

Teach them to give and take compliments assertively

Assertive compliment-sharing is a very important skill for confident people. In spite of the prevalent myth that if you are truly confident you should not need praise; compliments can be very useful motivating and encouraging additions to our children's own self-affirmations.

Toddlers know how to take compliments – they lap them up! If you praise their beautiful picture or their pretty dress they will usually beam a non-verbal 'thank-you' to you even if they don't articulate their thanks in words. But once they reach school age, many children will have learned to look coy and embarrassed at the mere hint of a compliment, and within a few more years they may be dismissing even much needed praise with 'polite' self-put-downs ('Well, it's not my best effort') or a 'retailiation' ('I think yours is much better'). You can point out this unnecessary dismissal of compliments and suggest that they just respond with a smile and thanks instead.

Encourage them also to give compliments generously, but watch out for any of the following common bad habits.

Giving compliments
Checklist of unassertive habits

- **Including a self-put-down** which takes away from the compliment (e.g. 'You're really clever at Maths – I'm always so hopeless.')
- **Including a put-down of the other person** ('That's great! It's a pity you didn't do it earlier.')
- **Throwing away the compliment** by slipping it unobtrusively into a conversation, or giving it at an inappropriate time or place. A common example of the latter is when people try to cheer someone up with an unwanted compliment. If a friend has just had a bad exam result and is upset, he or she may only want to hear empathic remarks ('It must be disappointing . . .') and may even find the compliment annoying ('. . . but don't worry, you're brilliant at Geography.')
- **Being too general** ('You look nice' rather than 'I like the way you've done your hair today, it seems to really suit you.')
- **Being too effusive,** which can evoke a cringe response

137

instead of a thank-you ('You're so brilliant at everything – you're totally amazing.')

- **Being indirect** by saying wonderful things about the person to other people, but not giving him or her direct praise ('I was telling Pete last night what a fantastic goal you scored.')

Finally, when encouraging your children to give their assertive compliments, let them know that the good news about compliment-sharing is that the more we give to others the more we are likely to receive in return!

Teach them how to give and take constructive criticism

This is the real testing area of confidence! While we cannot expect children to develop very sophisticated critical skills, we can encourage them to develop good rather than bad habits which they can build on later. Here are some basic tips to share with your children.

How to give criticism assertively

- **Choose the right moment**
  You could make this point if, for example, your child starts to criticize you when you are in public or when you are too busy to listen. You can then suggest an alternative time to talk.
- **Include something positive**
  You could suggest that they say something like 'I like playing with you, but when you . . .'.
- **Show consideration for the other person**
  Explain that people are more likely to take a criticism on board if we indicate that we have given some thought to 'their side of the story', e.g. 'I know it's difficult being the youngest, but . . .'.

- **Deal with one thing at a time**
  Help them to resist the temptation to bring up all their other dissatisfactions.
- **Don't use put-downs**
  You could point out when they are using these, and perhaps show them the list of examples that begins on pages 89–91.
- **Spell out the advantages of changing**
  Explain the 'home truth' that people are more likely to change if they can see that there may be an advantage for them – e.g. 'If you stop taking my things without asking, I won't mind letting you borrow them sometimes.'

How to receive criticism assertively

- **Think positively**
  Remind them that, although criticism hurts and the person giving it may be a 'baddie', we often learn something useful from it. This may help them to keep calm and listen attentively.
- **Keep calm**
  Teach them how to take control over their natural 'fight or flight' response when they perceive themselves as being under attack, by taking two or three slow deep breaths and making a conscious effort to relax any tension in their muscles.
- **Play for time**
  Help them resist the temptation to leap instantly to their own defence or retaliate, *especially* if they find what is being said very upsetting or unfair. When they get older, you could teach them the simple assertiveness technique called 'Fogging' which I describe below. At first they will find using this technique rather strange, as it will feel as though they are agreeing with their critic, but you could practise it together and they will soon realize just how

powerful and useful it can be. Even if they rarely use it, just knowing that they can cope with this kind of criticism will give them more confidence to be themselves and speak their mind even in the presence of 'know-alls' and bullies.

Fogging:

A technique for coping with unfair or unwanted criticism

Fogging can be used when:
- You want to play for time and give yourself a chance to calm down, think about what is being said and plan your response.
- Your critic has chosen the wrong time or place (e.g. in front of other friends or when you are just about to go off to a good party!).
- You are being criticized by someone whose opinion you don't need or want to hear (e.g. an unwanted 'friend' or acquaintance who just wants to hurt you).
- You know your critic is in 'a mood' and is being very obviously unfair, and you know it's not worth getting upset over what they are saying (e.g. a tired parent who is over-reacting!).

How it works:
- You respond (repeatedly, if necessary) to your critic by *appearing* to agree, indicating that there *could* be some truth in what he or she is saying (but inwardly telling yourself that your critic is wrong or that you'll think about it).

The result:
- the critic eventually gives up!

Examples of the fogging technique in action:
Note that the fogging words are in *italics* and the confidence-boosting self-talk is in brackets.

Critic A:	'You're always so mean – you never want to spend your money.'
Response:	'*Perhaps* I am mean.' (I know this is not true; I'm quite extravagant and generous when I choose to be so.)
Critic B:	'You never want to go out anywhere, you're so boring these days.'
Response:	'*Maybe* I don't go out as often as I used to.' (He's got a point; when I get home perhaps I ought to think about the way I'm spending my time.)
Critic C:	'You kids are all the same, you never care about anyone else, you've always got that music blasting the house out.'
Response:	'*Perhaps you're right*, the music *may* be a bit loud.' (She seems in a mood, she's having a go at everyone; I know she doesn't really mean it and I am considerate and the music is the same volume as always.)

EXERCISE: **Encouraging assertiveness**

- Together with your children work out a short concise Assertive Rights list which is meaningful for them and which you and others in the family feel is worthy of respect. During the next week, highlight when these rights are being respected and when they are not, and encourage your children, to do similarly (e.g. 'You haven't asked me', 'You're squashing my right to have ideas.'). If there is cause for debate – encourage an assertive style of debate!

- During the next week, make a contract with yourself to give your children some feedback on the compliments they share. If they are missing opportunities to give compliments, suggest what they could have said. ('Why not tell Sarah that you want to play with her because she's good fun?')

- Encourage your children to give you some constructive

criticism (e.g. about the way you read them a story, cooked a meal, etc.), helping them if necessary to give their feedback in an assertive style.

Remember:

> *Assertiveness is a positive and constructive alternative to passive or aggressive behaviour. It cannot always guarantee successful outcomes, but it does work wonders for the growth of self-esteem and mutual respect.*

Chapter 11

How to help your children manage their feelings

Being in control of our feelings is so closely linked to confidence that we often colloquially use the same word – 'cool' – to describe both states. Just consider its interchangeable meaning in these two sentences:

She looked so *cool* standing up there on stage.

He didn't get uptight. He was calm and *cool* about the problem.

Perhaps this synonymous link arose from the common misunderstanding that very confident people tend to be cold and emotionally detached. In truth, super-confident people enjoy their emotions and often experience them very deeply. They also have the capacity to express them freely and openly, but only generally do so after they have made a conscious decision to allow themselves to be spontaneous. Furthermore, every person whom I have met who has a problem with confidence also has at least one emotion which is out of his or her control.

Instead of trying to cover the whole range of different emotions which human beings are capable of feeling, I have decided that it would be more helpful to take a more general look at the subject.

In the process of helping myself and other people manage a whole variety of feelings more effectively, I have noticed that there are a number of common areas which always need to be worked on. I would suggest that each of these would also be useful for parents to focus on. I will now discuss each in turn and add some ideas of what practical action can be taken.

Awareness

Before children can be taught how to control their emotions they need to know that they are feeling them. This may sound obvious, but in fact in our society, where so much emphasis is given to living in our heads, children (girls as well as boys today) very quickly follow in their role-model's footsteps and can become quite detached from their emotions, even at a very young age. This is even more true for children who have experienced a series of traumas or who live in a particularly repressive atmosphere. They may find the degree of emotion they are feeling 'too hot to handle' and sense, rightly or wrongly, that the adults around them would too, so they soon learn automatically to protect themselves by firmly placing the unwanted or uncontrollable feeling into their subconscious. And nowadays who needs Freud or Hitchcock to tell us about the damage repressed feelings can do, especially if they manage to burst through the defences!

What can we do?

1. Ask our children regularly about their feelings.
2. Watch their body language for non-verbal indications of their feelings and feed this back to them, but without being too interpretive or making assumptions, for example:
   - 'I noticed you frowning – are you feeling worried?' (Rather than 'You're frowning – you must be worried.')
   - 'I heard you stamping upstairs, is there anything wrong?' (Rather than 'Why are you so mad?')

   'What you know in your head will not sustain you in moments

*of crisis . . . confidence comes from body awareness, knowing
what you feel in the moment.'*

Marion Woodman

3. Watch out for any changes in behaviour patterns which may
indicate that some feeling has been repressed. Note that I have
suggested a feeling in brackets, but although I have chosen
ones commonly underlying these symptoms, please
remember that it could be quite a different one or a mixture
of a few. For example:

- reluctance to go to bed or school (fear?)
- clinging to toy or comforter (sadness?)
- increase in obsessions and rituals (anxiety?)
- unusual disruptive or attention-seeking behaviour
  (jealousy?)
- fussy eating (worry?)
- increase in nail-biting, thumb-sucking or similar habits
  (helplessness?)
- frequent nightmares (nervousness?)
- bedwetting or soiling (loneliness?)
- persistent obsession with subjects like death or suicide
  (grief?)
- hyperactivity (boredom?)
- bullying and fighting over-aggressively (resentment?)
- daydreaming and failure to concentrate (depression?)
- lurid painting or drawing (anger?)

*'One cannot catch the meaning of a sullen look, a broad smile, or
a tearful face simply by listening . . . one must learn to catch the
meanings of a child's behaviour by "tuning in" to more than his
or her words.'*

Don Dinkmeyer and Gary D. McKay

Rights

Very often children become confused about whether or not
they should be having a particular feeling or degree of feeling,

because they have picked up messages from the world around them that this emotion is perhaps:

- insignificant ('I haven't got time to be worrying about little things like that.')
- nasty ('Nice children don't get cross when . . .')
- self-destructive ('You'll blow a gasket if you get so excited.')
- harmful to others ('You're giving me a headache carrying on like that.')
- socially isolating ('What do you think the neighbours would think if they heard you?')
- damaging to their esteem ('You are so soppy.')
- not authentic ('I know what you're really feeling.')
- too babyish ('Big boys don't get upset over silly things like that.')
- incomprehensible ('I don't understand why you should feel like that when . . .')

Children should not have their right to experience their emotions damaged or abused in these ways because the effect of doing so can do lasting damage to their confidence in themselves. *When children begin to question their right to feel, very often they begin to question their right to exist.*

What can we do?

1. We can make it clear to our children that they have a *right* to feel *any* emotion at *any* time in *any* place and with *any* person, even though they may choose, or be required, to subdue its expression temporarily – or may not immediately understand why they are feeling this.
2. Check our use of any responses which may be similar to those quoted above. (Many of these may be lodged in your auto-parent without your consent!)
3. Support them when anyone else abuses their right to feel their feelings.

Articulacy

Feelings are notoriously difficult to put into words. In fact, they may be better expressed through outlets such as music or art; nevertheless it is important that children learn how to express their emotions as accurately as possible in language that most people around them can understand. The mutual sharing of feelings is, after all, fundamental to those close intimate relationships which help us to feel of special value and help to underpin our self-confidence.

Articulacy is also important if we want to gain better control over our feelings. For example, anyone who, like myself, works with people who have problems with anger, depression or anxiety knows only too well that the first step is to help them to find more exact words to describe the degree of their feelings. This is the starting point for being able to monitor the escalation and de-escalation of feelings in response to certain situations, actions or people.

I'm not suggesting that it is necessary for you or your children to become a walking thesaurus, but it *is* important to have a reasonable degree of emotional articulacy.

How can we help?

1. Make a conscious effort to enrich the language we use ourselves to describe our feelings.
2. When our children use general words we can try to get them to be more specific by suggesting other words or phrases until the right one is found. In doing this you may well find that the feeling isn't actually what they, or you, thought it actually was. For example, the word 'frightened' can equal a little bit scared/scared stiff/worried/terrified/slightly anxious/sick inside/rumbling butterflies/overwhelmed/powerless/jealous, etc.
3. Play word games which will increase your children's emotional vocabulary. *Junior Scrabble* is an obvious one, but you could make up your own word-association one – which might transform an otherwise fraught car journey! Or you could use dull TV programmes for a 'spot the how many feelings' game. Whatever you do, don't make 'heavy weather' of this kind of activity, even though it has a very serious purpose, and remember that some children will always be better than others at learning and using vocabulary.

Responsibility

Perhaps one of the most important things you can do for your children with regard to their feelings is to help them take responsibility for them. Remember that in doing so you will be walking up a very steep hill! You will be challenging the prevalent but erroneous belief that very many of our emotional states are induced and controlled by forces outside ourselves. You may even be in the habit yourself of 'accusing' your children of *making* you happy/sad/annoyed/fed up or even murderously angry.

The reality is that no person, thing or situation has the power to make us feel a particular emotion, unless we allow him/her/it to do so.

Just think of two parents watching the same child drawing a wonderful big cat on the sitting room wall with a felt tip pen. Both may be equally horrified or both may be equally amused – on the other hand they could have opposite reactions. Each parent's emotional response to this display of rich talent will depend on very many variables, including his or her personality and the amount of food currently lodged in his or her stomach.

The belief that others can wield emotional control over us can be extremely damaging to children's confidence. It can lead them to depend too much on others, for example, to 'make' them feel strong or happy; it can also cause them to have little real trust in themselves because there will always be the lingering feeling that someone or something else has power over this most important aspect of themselves.

How can we help?

1. Help your children to view their feelings in a positive way (perhaps, for example, by treating their feelings with as much respect as you do their intellect). We can even help them see the negative ones as enriching, enlightening and healing, if we ourselves manage ours in a healthy way.
2. Keep a check on the language we use. For example, use language which doesn't put the onus on others for our feelings, such as:
   - 'I was very worried when you came home late.' (Instead of 'You worried me sick.')
   - 'I feel so proud of you.' (Instead of 'You make me very proud.')
   - 'I get embarrassed when you forget your table manners when we go out.' (Rather than 'Your lack of manners makes me cringe with embarrassment.')
   - 'I get upset when you leave your toys around.' (Instead of 'You and your toys all over the place are driving me mad.')

3. Help our children to change their language if they have picked up similar 'disowning' habits, while explaining our reasons for doing so.
4. Refuse to take on board any feelings they may try to transfer onto us as soon as they are old enough to understand what they are doing. For example when their irritation with the teacher or their younger brother finds its way to being expressed in a tantrum with you ('You make me go to school' or 'You gave birth to him.')

Release

If we encourage children to take responsibility for their feelings, we must also be prepared, if necessary, to help them learn and practise safe and constructive ways of releasing them.

When any of us begins to feel an emotion, an immediate chemical change takes place in our body which is designed to help us give some physical release to the feeling. For example:

- laughter and screams when we are happy or excited
- hugs and kisses when we feel loving
- giggles or blushes when we are embarrassed
- whimpers and tears when we feel sad or hurt
- shudders and screams when we are frightened
- growls and stamps when we are frustrated or angry.

The vast majority of young children have no problem expressing their feelings, but cultural conditioning soon dampens the spontaneity of most. Of course, if they are going to live comfortably in our society, it is quite appropriate that it should do so to a certain degree.

But to what degree? I find very frequently on my confidence courses that many people simply do not know when it is appropriate to bring the emotional 'soft pedal' into action. They know that they are continually using it ineptly because of the adverse reactions they meet, but they have very little idea of how to use it 'correctly'. In our society it is all too often assumed that children will learn emotional skills quite automatically through watching others, or through trial and error. The result is that very many children miss out, either because their role-models are not skilled themselves or because they are exposed to a confusing mixture of norms and rules from various cultures (e.g. school versus home; home versus the childminder's family or even Dad versus Mum.)

Although we cannot completely protect children from making social 'gaffes' with their feelings, or copying the very many adults who over-repress their spontaneity, we nevertheless have a responsibility to guide them with whatever wisdom we do have; at the very least this will raise their awareness of the importance of emotional release.

What can we do?

1. Let them know that releasing feelings is natural and energizing and that holding them back too much and too often can damage both mental and physical health. Using examples from their own experience if you can, show them that, for example:

   - headaches can be caused by unreleased frustration
   - blocked sinuses by unshed tears
   - stomach cramps by unexpressed excitement or anxiety
   - a fight between two people can escalate due to a build-up of unreleased anger
   - a panic attack brought on by unexpressed fear
   - depression caused by repressed irritation or boredom.

   (If you feel a little out of your depth with regard to knowledge on this subject there are many books now available to help you. Some are recommended in the Further Reading section of this book. If, however, you feel like you are drowning in the deep end, you could seek the help of a professional counsellor or join a self-help group.)

2. Teach them that, in certain situations, we have to *postpone* or subdue the physical release of our feelings so that we can get on with what we need to do or so that we do not offend, hurt or annoy certain other people. (Which situations you choose to specify will, of course, depend on the age and personality of your child, the culture he or she lives in and the values you have chosen to live by.)
3. Encourage and show them how to let go of feelings in a safe place and suggest ways in which they can do this (e.g. banging cushions, screaming into a pillow, playing an aggressive game, singing, dancing, etc.)

Control

We have already discussed how important it is for children to be aware that they may need to curb the expression of their feelings. It is also important to give them some guidance on how to regain physical control until they can find a safe or appropriate place to release their feelings. This may involve *teaching* them how to calm themselves down – rather than just telling them to do so!

What can we do?

1. Experiment with doing calming activities together and notice which is most effective with each of your children. You may find that a walk relaxes one but excites another, or that one brilliant piece of music will work wonders with everyone.
2. Teach them some simple relaxation and breathing exercises, but remember to give them plenty of practice. Any book on stress management will give you a number to choose from, but if you are short of ideas you will find some interesting ones for young children in David Lewis's book *Helping Your Anxious Child* (see Further Reading list).
3. Help them to use their imagination to conjure up images which will, by association, help them instantly to get into

the emotional state they need or want to be in. Try to use images which are very personal and meaningful to each individual child. For example:

relaxation: – a floppy rag doll lying on a bed
                – ducks swimming in the local park
                – a favourite pet sunning itself on the lawn
courage: – Superwoman or Superman flying through the air
                – the family cat arching its back
                – Martin Luther King giving a speech

When you have some time to help children prepare for an occasion when they may need extra control over their feelings, you can use the technique called 'Guided Fantasy'. This will help to 'programme' their mind with an image of themselves in complete emotional control. Here is an example.

Using a guided fantasy

Purpose

To help your children prepare emotionally for an event which you or they think may be hard for them to handle and throughout which you want to help them remain calm and confident. (e.g. an exam, match, party, start at new school, facing up to teasing from a bully, asking a question in class, etc.)

How to do it

Suggest that your child lies down and closes his or her eyes. You can use some quiet music or put on a cassette of soothing sounds (bird-song, for example.) Now spend five minutes or so helping him or her to become deeply physically relaxed.

Once you sense he or she is feeling very calm, and using a gentle voice, talk your child through the event as though it were happening in the present. Ask your child to use his or her imagination to create a mental picture of him- or herself doing whatever he or she has to do, calmly and confidently. It is often helpful to start the visualization at the beginning of the day in question, so that your child has an image of him- or herself waking up in a positive mood and remaining calm throughout the time leading up to the event. The amount of detail you use and the length of time you take for the visualization must depend on the age and personality of each child, but I would suggest that you need at least 10 minutes for it to be effective.

Although bedtime is an obvious time to do this exercise, you may find that when your child is tired he or she cannot relax so easily. In this case it is probably better to do it earlier in the day, but then to remind him or her of their visualization just before bedtime.

Example

'Imagine that it is now Tuesday. You are waking up in the morning and you remember that it is the day you take your test . . . you feel pleased because you have worked really hard and you know that you are going to do well . . . now it's a few minutes before the exam . . . so you are taking some nice long deep breaths and you are feeling very calm and confident . . . watch yourself writing away . . . you are doing fine even though one of the questions seemed very difficult at first . . . now you have finished . . . look how pleased you are that you did so well and that you kept so calm and confident all the way through.'

EXERCISE: **Managing feelings**

- Imagine an 'everyday' situation in which your child is likely to experience fear (e.g. entering a new class at school, going to a first disco, etc). Using the checklist above as a guide, note down what you could say to help:
  - clarify your child's awareness of the feeling
  - show respect for his or her right to experience the feeling
  - articulate his or her experience of the feeling
  - take responsibility for the feeling
  - encourage safe expression of the tension
  - take control of the physical symptoms

- Repeat the above, focussing on a situation in which your child could feel, or has felt:
  - grief
  - intense excitement
  - jealousy
  - anger

- To familiarize yourself with the technique, practise using the Guided Fantasy with your child, explaining how you would then both know how to use it when and if you needed to.

'All our emotions are nothing but a flurry of biochemical reactions in our brains and we can spark them off at any moment. But first we must learn how to take control of them consciously instead of living in reaction.'

Anthony Robbins

'We know too much and feel too little.'

Bertrand Russell

Chapter 12
Positive problem-solving

'A carefree childhood is a happy childhood'

– Do you agree or disagree?

Maybe you would want to qualify this rather glib generalization, but I would suggest that most of us do harbour this belief somewhere in our subconscious, because it is so firmly embedded in modern parenting culture. Because of it, for example, we may feel it is our duty to protect our children from even the ordinary stresses of everyday life, so we censor our discussion of our worries in their presence or give them more expensive presents than our real budgets can afford.

'You can't be brave if you've only had wonderful things happen to you.'

Mary Tyler Moore

Of course, no parents wish their children's early years to be totally overwhelmed with problems over which they have no control, because we all know how important a basic sense of security is to the development of mental health. But equally, a childhood totally devoid of hassle is hardly an ideal psychological preparation for living in our undeniably complicated and unfair world.

As a therapist I have a number of serious reservations about the 'carefree childhood' myth because I have seen so much evidence that it can lead to:

- over-protectiveness, which denies children the opportunity to learn how to cope with problems
- the suppression of children's creative potential, which is so often stimulated by a desire to find new solutions to problems
- the pretence that life is, or can be, problem free – when it plainly is not. This kind of denial can leave children wondering whether there is something wrong with them for having the fears or worries they are experiencing.
- the development of the emotionally unhealthy habit of repressing negative feelings
- the postponement of problem-solving until an overwhelming crisis point is reached and both child and parent feel (perhaps justifiably) totally inadequate to cope
- stifling of positive parenting potential in parents who are plainly providing a 'good-enough' childhood for their children, but who feel constantly inadequate and subsequently become over-anxious or resentful.

It is neither the quality nor the quantity of problems that children encounter which knocks their confidence and damages their mental health, but the way in which such problems are handled.

So how can we best help our children to use the difficulties they encounter constructively? Obviously, a very important way is to be a *model* of perfect problem-solving ourselves! Yet even this is often not quite enough, and indeed, our own competency may in fact sometimes be counter-productive – first because we are so clever, courageous, persistent, creative, etc. that we may find it too temptingly easy to rush in and solve our children's difficulties, and secondly because our children may be blinded into inaction by our shining example.

As parents wanting to help our children develop in this area, there are important ways in which we can help them.

'Avoiding danger is no safer in the long run than outright exposure. The fearful are caught as often as the bold.'

Helen Keller

1. Maintaining a positive attitude

This is particularly important if your child appears to be losing his or her confidence in the ability to solve problems, or if you have a tendency to get over-anxious or over-protective or sweep too many 'nasties' under the carpet.

You could take steps to keep your auto-parent in a positive frame of mind by regularly repeating to yourself the following phrases and then using them as supportive self-talk when you see your child 'suffering' with a problem.

- Children can be emotionally healed of any trauma if it is handled positively and constructively.
- Children can be psychologically strengthened through experience of coping with difficulties.
- Children can learn invaluable survival skills through the process of problem-solving.

2. Keeping our involvement appropriate

Problem-solving is best learned, like any other skill, by taking graduated steps forward, so that each success increases our confidence to cope with the next slightly more difficult one. While we cannot always dictate the pace at which problems flow into our children's lives, we can often dictate the amount of responsibility we allow them to take for solving their own various difficulties.

'Too often we give children answers to remember rather than problems to solve.'

Roger Lewin

When our children are babies, we obviously take the major responsibility for their problems, but by the time they reach late adolescence our role should have *gradually* developed into that of being a wise observer who is consulted only when help and support are required. The pace of this process must always be determined by the maturity and aptitude of each individual child and the nature of the particular problem encountered. We may therefore find ourselves helping one child more than we helped his or her siblings at the same age. Each child has a unique personality and differing levels of experience and stress in his or her life. (For example, assumptions about the problem-solving skills of the youngest in a family or of handicapped children are often too readily made, partly because they tend to put on an act of being more mature and competent than they actually are.)

So, before starting to help a child, put aside your memories of how Billy or Angie (or even you) coped with a similar problem, and ask yourself the following kinds of questions:

• Does this problem entirely belong to the child, or do I or others have some responsibility for solving it or part of it?

- What degree of skill or experience does this particular child bring to this particular problem?
- What chance of success would he or she have if left alone with this problem? (You can use a 1–10 scale as a guide if this helps).

3. Being supportive

Even if we have decided to take a big step into the background and let our child work out his or her own solutions, we still have an important supportive role to play. We can encourage, be a shoulder to cry or lean on, or simply give an assurance that we're waiting in the wings for the celebration or commiseration.

Hopefully you already have the kind of relationship with your children which gives them the impression that you are rooting for them and will be there for them whatever the outcome – but can you afford always to take it for granted? When children are feeling very anxious about a problem they can, and often do, 'forget' we are there for them. This is especially true when they are feeling 'stupid' because they are trying to solve a 'minor' problem which everyone else in the world appears to have mastered. (Remember your struggle with shoelaces?)

So while your children are engaged in trying to solve whatever problem it is that they have, ask yourself if you have clearly communicated your support to them by, for example:

- empathizing with their feelings ('I can see that it's worrying/frightening/exciting, etc.)
- giving them a smile, hug or squeeze of the hand
- bringing them a cool drink or a cup of tea
- sending them a good-luck card or note
- telling them that you will make time to be with them, if they need you or want you
- showing them the entry in your diary or the family calendar for their special occasion.

4. Teaching problem-solving strategies

Most adults have their own favourite problem-solving strategies even though they may not give them that name. They may be referred to as 'common sense' or 'tricks of the trade', 'grandma's secret of success' or 'my funny habit', or even 'what I learned the hard way was . . .'.

What many people forget, however, is that children are not born with this kind of wisdom, even if it does feel like second nature to us and in this busy day and age, we are not so readily available to pass on our tried and tested strategies. So make sure that you take time a) to clarify your strategies to yourself and translate them into terms which your children can readily understand and b) to share the secret!

If you feel that you yourself need some extra problem-solving strategies, there are many good books now on the market which could be of help. In my earlier book *The Positive Woman* there are several simple strategies which you could use, particularly with older children (e.g. Brainstorming, Mind Mapping and FACE THE FACTS). Other good sources of problem-solving strategies can be found in the books of Tony Buzan and Edward de Bono (see the Further Reading list) and the many self-help books on specific problem areas.

For the time being, here is a new strategy called 'START' which you may like to try. I have devised it to help you to get a child who is feeling overwhelmed or over-anxious to take some constructive steps forward along the problem-solving road. It will also help your child to look at the challenge in a positive way, especially as it suggests a reward at the end. It can be used equally well with small problems and larger, more complex issues. You could start using it on a problem you may share with a child, so you can begin by working together and then work towards encouraging him or her to use it on his or her own.

'Procrastination is the thief of time.'

Edward Young

START can be used as the basis for an informal talk or a written action plan. (Remember that research has proved that we are much more likely to do the things which we have committed ourselves to do on paper!)

In the following section I will introduce each step and then give you some examples of the strategy in action.

START: A problem-solving strategy for children

The word START is made up of the first letters of the five words which can be used to help children remember five important steps in solving a problem both confidently and successfully..

S	T	A	R	T
P	H	C	E	R
E	I	T	V	E
A	N		I	A
K	K		E	T
			W	

Speak

'A problem shared is a problem halved.'

This proverb is another bit of worldly wisdom that we must make sure our children reap some benefit from. Too many children keep their problems to themselves or 'act them out' (e.g. hitting out at a younger brother, refusing to go to bed, vandalizing school property, etc.). So the first step is to encourage them to *talk about* whatever is worrying or concerning them to someone else with whom they feel comfortable. In most instances this person is likely to be you, but if their problem *is* you, or for some reason they cannot share it with you, encourage them to speak to someone else – even if that means letting off steam to your partner, a friend, Grandma or a teacher.

Hopefully, whomever they choose to talk to will be someone who will also give them hope and encourage and help them to take steps to solve the problem, but you may need to explain that they may meet a few people in the world who have not read this chapter!

Think

This step is to help children remember to give themselves some quiet time to think about all the different aspects of their problem before deciding what to do or not do. You can suggest, or remind them of, practical ways in which they may be able to clarify their thoughts and come up with new ideas. These may vary enormously with the age and ability of your child, but could include, for example:

- drawing a picture
- making 'good things' and 'bad things' lists
- representing the above in more concrete terms using toys and objects as symbols
- improvising a play or making up a story about the problem with different endings
- using brainstorming or mind-mapping techniques
- going to the library to do some research and to make notes.

By encouraging them to engage in one of these 'thinking activities' you will be helping your children to learn how to switch out of their emotional 'child' mode and move into their 'adult' mode, which is the most appropriate part of our personality for problem-solving (remember the discussion in Chapter 2 on personality?) Most children get a big boost to their confidence when they make this switch because they feel instantly more 'grown up' and less powerless.

Act

'A problem that is well formulated is half resolved.'
                                                              Charles Kettering

The next stage involves helping your children to make a practical action plan which should clearly spell out the following:

- **the long-term goal** – this will summarize concisely the desired outcome, but don't forget it must be an achievable objective and be given a realistic timescale.
- **short-term goals** – these are vital because even adults are more likely to follow through on an action plan if they can take some small step forward *immediately*. Keep these goals very concrete so that the achievement is easily measurable – and be careful not to have too many.

Review

Even the most highly self-disciplined among us usually work more diligently at solving a problem if our progress is being monitored by someone who genuinely cares about us an the outcome. (This is the principle behind successful problem-solving groups such as Weight-Watchers and Alcoholics Anonymous, and is now being used in some schools as well).

Remember, however, that nagging or too rigid a surveillance from parents can be counter-productive. So, after explaining the supportive benefits of some kind of review (maybe by sharing an example from your own experience), you will have to work out with your children what kind of check on their progress would be most helpful. If they would prefer someone else to help them in this way (e.g. a friend, a teacher or their other parent), make sure that they include making contact with this person as part of their action plan.

Encourage them also to do their own reviewing by suggesting practical ways of doing this, such as making notes in a diary, putting up a graph on their bedroom wall, or using a star chart or brightly coloured stick-on reminder notes.

Treat

This is the stage when you plan a reward for either solving the problem or, very importantly, for 'good effort' in the event of slow progress or failure. Although working on some problems can be fun and rewarding in itself, I don't believe we should ever count on it being continually so. More often than not we go through a despairing stage when even the achievement of our short-term goals seems impossible and our confidence starts ebbing away. So, although having a treat in store does not always work like a magic carrot, a reminder from time to time that it is there can be be very inspiring for most children.

When planning the treats make sure that they are appropriate and not 'over the top'. For many children the promise of spending some special time with a beloved parent is very effective; others might need something more concrete to focus on, such as a jar of mounting coins towards the purchase of a desired item.

Always try to ensure that the child receives the treat, even if arriving at the solution of the problem seems rewarding enough in itself. The habit of giving ourselves regular rewards is so essential to confidence-building and -boosting that I'm convinced it is better to err on the side of too many rather than too few.

Examples of how to use the START strategy

Please note that the following are merely illustrations of how to use the strategy. They are not intended to be used as guidelines on how to tackle similar problems should your child experience them, because each situation and child must be treated individually.

Problem A: Underachievement

A 10-year-old son is upset by his report, which has stated that this term he is underachieving at school and appears to have lost confidence in his ability.

Speak
His parents could encourage him to talk about his feelings (of despair? anger?) and tell him about a time when they felt similarly and how that affected their work. As they talk, it emerges that he feels very inadequate beside his older brother.

Think

His parents might help him to:

- make a list of his 'best times' and 'worst times'.
- note when he first began to lose confidence in his ability to do well. Was it connected to any significant event? (E.g. when his elder brother moved to the senior school/when Mum changed her job/when he wasn't selected for the football team, etc.).
- note down which subjects he is good at, and which subjects he is not, and think how these compare with his brother's strengths and weaknesses.
- look at how he feels and performs with different teachers.

Act

Long-term goal: 5 per cent improvement on his grades by the time the next report is issued.

Short-term actions:

- speak to brother tomorrow about how he feels and ask for his help with Maths
- make new homework timetable at week-end
- write out list of six best achievements and make into colourful poster for his bedroom, leaving space to add new ones every so often
- Mum or Dad to make appointment on Monday to talk to year head about extra help at school and to see English teacher

Review

- Talk about progress every Saturday after breakfast, and add any new achievements to the poster.
- See teachers again in six weeks' time.

Treat

- Family trip to to theme park or football match with brother.

Problem B: Being Teased for Wearing Glasses

A six-year-old daughter, since being prescribed glasses, appears to be becoming much more shy and unwilling to go to other people's houses.

Speak

While expressing feelings about having to wear glasses, it might emerge that she has been persistently teased.

Think

Her parents could help her to:

- recall which particular 'silly' or 'unkind' children have teased her, and count up all the many others who haven't.
- list all the nice people they know who wear glasses.
- think of all the different things these people might say if someone teased them.

Act

Long-term goal: By Christmas, have grown enough in courage to be able to wear glasses every day and ignore any silly teasing or bullying.

Short-term actions:

- tomorrow, practise answering back the bullies (e.g. role-playing with Mum or Dad, or doing a little play with friends).
- buy a little teddy with glasses on to put in her pocket to talk to and give her extra courage (or draw a picture of one to have by her bed).
- during the next week, wear glasses just for a little longer each day.
- if teasing hasn't reduced within a month, Mum or Dad to talk to parents or teachers.

Review

- Tell Mum or Dad each time someone teases.
- A coin is put in a jar for each extra hour that she wears her glasses over the next month.

Treat

After a month Mum and Dad will double the amount of money in the jar and take her to the shops so she can choose something special to spend it on.

Problem C: Anxiety Following Bereavement

An eight-year-old son has been having nightmares and is getting very over-cautious – even crossing the road is becoming an ordeal. He insists on having the light on at night, which concerns his parents because he is due to go away with the Cubs on a camping holiday.

Speak

His parents could encourage him to talk about all the things he is frightened of, while sharing some of the fears which they had as children. Prompted by them, he might begin also to talk about his Grandpa's death a few months before and they might find out that this had set off a real fear of ghosts and a general anxiety about death.

Think

They could then help him to:

– make a list of some special memories of Grandpa.
– think about what Grandpa would have said if he had met a ghost in his room.
– think about the things and people that help him to feel safe and forget about his fears of death.

Act

Long-term goal: to go to the Cub camp.
Short-term actions:

– frame the list of special memories of Grandpa together with a photo and put in sitting room, say goodnight to picture before going to bed.
– tomorrow night have the light off for 10 minutes, stay awake but with eyes closed imagine his room filled with the 'safe' things and people.
– repeat the 'lights off' procedure each night for a week or 10 days, adding five minutes each night.

Review

Make a small chart to put by the bed on which you and he can note his progress either day by day or week by week.

Treat

Buy something special to take on the Cubs camping holiday.

Problem D: Loneliness and Social Isolation

A 14-year-old daughter has fallen out with her best friend over a month ago and is now becoming worryingly reclusive.

Speak

Someone (parents or friend) could help her to talk about her feelings of anger at being let down and encourage her to cry about her loss. Daughter reveals that she now gets very panicky about going to the club or anywhere that this girl and her new friends might be.

Think

They could then:

- list all the good things and bad things about that friendship.
- think about what kind of friendship she needs now.
- think about whether there is anyone else at school or in the club whom she would like to know better.

Act

Long-term goal: new friend or friends by next term.
Short-term actions:
- go out once a week.
- make an assertive rights poster (see page 133).
- do some relaxation exercises and try a *guided visualization* tape to help her gather courage for end-of-term disco.

Review

Talk again in a month.

Treat

A trip to city shops for new skirt for disco.

EXERCISE: **Problem-solving**

- List three major problems which you have had in your life. Beside each note down: a) any unexpected positive outcome from the experience and b) anything you feel you learned from dealing with that problem.
- Practise applying the START strategy, either to a real problem which your child has currently or to a hypothetical one which you fear he or she could encounter.

'Problems are opportunities in work clothes.'

Henry J. Kaiser

Chapter 13
Dealing with conflict

'The way I see it, if you want the rainbow you gotta put up with the rain.'

Dolly Parton

– and, if you truly want confident children, you gotta put up with the conflict!

We can turn our conflicts with our children into confidence-building opportunities. Most people see (and perhaps experience) only the very real negative potential of conflicts for destroying self-esteem and loving relationships. If you have already started to put into practice the philosophy and ideas outlined in the rest of this book, you will, I hope, have a much more positive attitude about your conflicts with your children and they should already feel much easier to handle and be much more constructive in their outcome.

In relation to confidence-building, when we are in conflict with our children there are three important questions we need to ask ourselves continually:

1. Is the background atmosphere conducive to constructive resolution?
2. Are crises being managed with strength and skill?
3. Are resolutions routinely negotiated with justice and sensitivity?

Conducive atmosphere

Anyone who is bringing up children according to the basic principles already discussed in this book is likely to be on the right environmental track. There are a number of key characteristics we would expect to note in such a family:

– respect for individuality
– mutual empathy
– self-awareness
– tolerance of imperfections
– freedom to make mistakes
– willingness to consider change
– positive thinking
– effective stress management
– clear values, rules and responsibilities
– direct assertive communication
– open expression of well-managed feelings
– strategic problem-solving

As you read this list, do you have an image of home or of an enviable heaven?

Even if you haven't quite reached the clouds, at least your children will know that you are trying, and their confidence will be boosted anyway by being part of a 'team' which is working together in the right spirit and towards a shared ideal. As they get older, they can be encouraged to take more and more responsibility for helping to maintain an atmosphere where conflicts can be dealt with openly and positively. I have found that my children are very astute observers of falling standards, and these are often revealed during a time of conflict. ('Aren't people allowed to make mistakes anymore?' or 'I thought we were supposed to say what we feel.') Getting adults to eat humble pie from time to time must be good for a relatively powerless child but, to make sure that no one gets too sanctimonious, you could pin the following quote up on the kitchen wall!

'It is reasonable to have perfection in our eye that we may always advance toward it, though we know it can never be reached.'

Samuel Johnson

Crisis management

Crises are always uncomfortable, but they can be very positive. I understand that the Chinese word for crisis is made up of two characters: one representing 'danger' and the other, 'opportunity'!

Conflict crises between parents and children can take many differing forms, from toddler tantrums in the supermarket to teenage hysterics about curfews in front of the vicar. There is no magic formula for coping with these, but if we respect the following four basic general rules we can ride through most storms without *anyone's* confidence being seriously dented.

1. Keep control of anger
2. Avoid giving, or threatening, punishment

3. Postpone resolution of differences
4. Authoritatively state needs and set out clear choice

Let's now consider each of these rules in turn.

Keeping control of anger

Some degree of anger, be it mild irritation or furious rage, is an inevitable accompaniment to conflict crisis. And, although I am a great 'fan' of this much feared and maligned emotion (because I value its natural healing and self-protective functions), I do believe anger must be handled with *extreme* care when the diagreement is between an adult and a child. Even children who are physically strong enough to defend themselves against an angry parent cannot be expected to have the emotional strength or same degree of behavioural skill with which to cope with this difficult emotion. Therefore – *it is vital that, as parents, we accept a major part of the responsibility for the way anger is handled by* both parties *during a conflict*.

If, during a conflict, either your or your children's anger habitually feels difficult to control, I would suggest that you do some extra self-development work in this area. My book *Managing Anger* sets out a model for handling this emotion in an assertive, safe manner and includes many exercises and strategies designed to help you take more effective control, and to encourage others to do similarly. Here is an example of one of the strategies which you could use to help you and your children calm down if you should find that either or both of your tempers are escalating during a conflict.

'Don't Get Too Boiling' Strategy

i	r	e	r
s	o	n	e
t	u	s	a
a	n	i	t
n	d	o	h
c		n	e
e			

The first letters of each of the words in this phrase can be used as a reminder of the four steps to take.

Distance

Immediately you feel that a physiological anger response has taken place in either you or your child, you should concentrate on keeping a safe distance from each other if at all possible – until you are both calm. Think of anger as being contagious, because when it occurs in one person, the other *is* much more likely to get a similar feeling (even if he or she turns it inwards it can still be destructive). But make sure that your child does not think you have deserted him or her, or he or she is likely to view this step as a punishment. This will mean making sure you are still within sight or hearing of a young child and that you only keep your distance until you have calmed down.

What exact steps you will take to establish this distance will vary with the child and your environment, but it could mean, for example:

- passing a baby to another person to hold
- putting a toddler in a playpen or distant corner of a room
- separating yourself from a young child by a door with safety glass in
- asking your partner to take over while you go for a walk
- sending a teenager to his or her room for an hour.

If it is not possible to separate yourself physically, try to do so emotionally. This next step could help you.

Ground

The object of this step is to bring the angry person 'back down to earth'. You can do this by taking a strong physical grip of some inanimate object which feels steady and secure and will show your child that you are in a fixed position. (Your child will learn to imitate this behaviour from your example.)

Alternatively, or additionally, focus your thoughts on something mundane (e.g. counting the blue objects in the room, or encouraging your child to do the time-honoured trick of counting to 10.)

Tension

It is important to remember that it is the build-up of tension with anger that makes it such a dangerous emotion. So it is important that you find a safe, non-destructive way of releasing this tension. This can be done, for example, by:

- articulating the feeling, using a strong voice and colourful (but not necessarily aggressive) language if the setting permits
- growling and screaming if the room is adequately sound-proofed
- stamping your feet, shaking your wrists and stretching (i.e. actions which are *non-threatening*)
- hitting a punchbag or kicking a football or cushion

Whenever your children try to release tension in a destructive way, instead of just telling them to stop, show them a safe alternative.

Breathe

Once the tension has been released it is important to bring your body back to its 'decompressed' state. The best way to do this in a crisis is to take some slow, deep breaths. This will be even more effective if, at the same time, you can visualize a peaceful scene. You could remind your child of a favourite personal relaxation symbol (see page 153) or encourage him or her to engage in an activity which you know has a calming effect. You will need to experiment to find whatever suits you and your child, but I know that when I am angry, listening to quiet soothing music has no effect, whereas cleaning the kitchen works wonders!

Avoiding punishment

Whatever your views on the merits of punishment, try to avoid meting it out in the heat of the crisis because, if you do use it, at its best it is likely to be ineffective and, at its worst, aggressively destructive. (Even 'the light slap' falls into this category and has earned its curative reputation merely on the strength of its power to relieve parental tension rather than having a beneficial effect on dissenting children.)

Remember that your main aim is to bring both parties to a rational, calm state of mind so that you can resolve the conflict effectively. Using your greater strength or resources to punish a relatively powerless child *before* resolution will only fuel the child's anger or send him or her into a paralytic state of fear or choked-up resentment.

Equally, we should always refrain from threatening punishment because they are more often than not ignored and they are likely to be 'over-the-top'. Even the threats I hear made in public places, which so often contain demeaning put-downs or frightening possibilities, can only damage confidence. ('You're not worth bothering about, I shall just ignore you for the rest of the journey' or 'When we get home, I'll see you'll never try that on again.') I dread to think what may be said, or done, in the privacy of these families' homes.

'The fault no child ever loses is the one he was most punished for.'
Cesare Beccaria (1738–1794!)

Postponing resolution

Children will always demand an instant solution, and many stressed parents seek one too – but, as a rule, this is rarely possible because democratic conflict resolution takes time and requires calm, rational minds to think and talk through the issues.

So play for time by using an *empathy statement* ('I know that you want to . . .'/'I can see that you're upset but . . .') and the Broken Record technique (see page 135) to repeat calmly and persistently over and over again that you will talk about 'it' later, while '. . . for the time being this (or that) is what is going to happen.'

Stating needs and giving choices

Assertive expressions of needs and choices are the alternatives to the pathetic pleas, desperate demands and empty threats that many of us use in the process of trying to discipline our children. They need to be expressed concisely in an authoritative, but friendly, tone of voice and should be repeated calmly over and over again, without responding to argument, until the child has complied or clearly understood the consequences of non-compliance. Using the child's 'normal' name (and not a name reserved especially for angry moments) shows respect and adds impact.

Here are some examples of what might be said after both parties have calmed down. Note that empathy statements and promises of a future negotiation have also been included.

- 'John, I know you feel it is unfair, and we will talk again tomorrow, but you must go to bed now. You have the choice of going up on your own or being carried.'
- 'Katie, I know that you are in the middle of watching a programme, but your room needs tidying now because (as I said earlier) I am doing the hoovering this morning. You can do it now and have a clean room or leave it to get dirtier and dirtier.'
- 'Ben, although I know you feel frustrated, I am not going to talk about what happens in Jim's family now. Tonight I want you to return by eight o'clock. You can agree to come back at that time now or not go out tonight. We will talk about it further at the week-end.'

'It may not be immediately obvious, but discipline and being strict can be a form of loving and caring. Children need to know what is right and wrong and need to have clear limits set on their behaviour.'

Dr John Pearce

Just negotiations

'Children need love, especially when they do not deserve it.'
Harold S. Herbert

As adults we must always remember that we are likely to have the edge on children when we are negotiating the resolution of a conflict with them. We must make allowances for the fact that they will not:

– be as articulate as we are
– be as skilled at controlling feelings
– be self-aware enough to understand the reasons behind their feelings or behaviours
– have enough experience of life to appreciate the consequences of some actions or attitudes
– appreciate the value of conciliatory gestures or apologies

This means that we are not equal partners at the negotiating table and that we may have to *give more than we take* – even after we have shared our superior wisdom and taught our child the necessary social skills.

More specifically, if we are concerned about using conflicts to promote children's confidence, as well as finding resolutions, even when we are talking to teenagers we must generally be prepared to do the following:

• Make the first move and suggest a talk.
• Be the first to offer an apology.
• Indicate that we have respect for their feelings and position and genuinely want to hear their point of view, including a positive comment or observation if possible (e.g. 'I know that when we have had disagreements in the past, you have come up with some good ideas' or 'I know that you are concerned about your brother as well.').
• Encourage them to express safely their negative feelings towards us, before coming in with our criticisms.

- Describe the problem in an objective, non-threatening way (e.g. 'There appears to be a misunderstanding about/clash of interests over . . .') and ask them if they agree.
- Ask questions or make suggestions (based on our *guesses*) which may help our children to understand the less obvious causes behind the conflict (e.g. loneliness, the generation gap, jealousy, boredom, confused communication, etc.).
- Help our children to articulate their arguments and suggestions in an assertive style if they lapse into aggressive behaviour or are too passive.
- Defend, in understandable but non-patronizing language, our non-negotiable rules and values and also clearly spell out the consequences of non-compliance (and be prepared to follow through on these consistently).
- Demonstrate how to apologize for mistakes and how to back down with good grace from arguments when these have been proved to be illogical, unfair or out-of-date.
- Show our children how they can make amends if they have hurt someone or destroyed something.
- Draw the negotiation to a positive conclusion when either party becomes too tired or emotional to continue and suggest a continuance if necessary. ('Well, I'm pleased that we have started to talk, let's continue in the morning when we have both had some more time to think.').
- Do the 'final summary' outlining any new agreement or redefining the status quo and spelling out what everyone has learned and gained from the conflict.

EXERCISE: **Dealing with conflict**

- Reflect on one particular conflict you have recently had with your child. Could it have been handled more positively and constructively? Re-read this chapter slowly, making notes as you go along to give you ideas about how you might have handled the situation differently.
- Discuss conflict problems with your partner or friends, asking them for feedback on your ideas.

- If your child is old enough, have a talk with him or her about your conclusions, and try to negotiate a better way of handling a similar situation should it occur in the future.
- With your child, make a poster of the 'Don't Get Too Boiling' strategy and pin it up somewhere prominent. Remind each other to use it!

'Fighting is far better than pretending that you are not divided.'

M. Scott Peck

Chapter 14
The flight to the outside world

'There are only two lasting bequests we can hope to give to our children. One of these is roots; the other, wings.'

Hodding Carter

Most of this book has been concerned with how to give our children the 'roots' to which Hodding Carter refers. One chapter is left to talk about the wings!

If parents are emotionally healthy themselves, and have done an effective job in establishing the 'roots' of childrens' confidence, the wings will grow quite naturally at the right pace for each child. Nevertheless there are a number of steps we can take to ensure that our children's flight into the world outside is as smooth as possible – even if we have no real control over its path or the storms it may be destined to meet on the horizon.

Here are some of the main steps which we as parents can take to help our children use their wings with super-confidence.

Be an inspiring model

Our first responsibility is, of course, to help make the outside world seem an exciting and attractive place to be flying into – this is yet another area in which our actions will speak very much louder than any words. If our children experience us as people who have confidence in the world and enjoy its challenges, as well as its safe, pretty havens, they will be inspired to test it for themselves.

Widen the horizon

Do not confine your children's image of the world to their own nest for too long. Instead, make sure that you:

- take them into the adult world with you as much as possible
- bring a variety of new people into your home as often as possible
- if your life is relatively sheltered, provide at the very least, second-hand experience of other families, towns or cultures – through, for example, books and TV
- arrange visits or 'work experience' to places/situations they have shown an inclination to work in eventually. (Don't rely on the school to do all this, because their funds and contacts will be limited.)
- make travel a high priority when planning your budget
- involve them (personally if possible) in community or world issues

Handle separations positively

From the moment that we start playing 'peek-a-boo' with our babies we are preparing them for separation – a process which should continue to take place at a slow, step-by-step pace until our children are confident and competent enough to survive in the world independently.

In an ideal world, the pace of this separation would be adjusted to each individual child, but our modern-day reality is that our children have to conform to the norms of society's timetable. For example, there are general expectations and even laws about the age at which they are expected to start or finish school. Children who have difficulty in conforming to the 'separation timetable' of the world around them are often thought to 'have a problem' (a label which can only have a negative impact on their confidence). The truth is that in the vast majority of instances when this occurs it is actually the *parents* who have the problem, and not the children – it is they who cannot manage the very natural anxiety that occurs with separation.

Assuming that the reason this may happen is not because you are clinging to your children to satisfy your own needs, but are simply floundering a little because you are not sure how to handle the situation, what can you do?

Firstly you must re-establish confidence in your own ability to understand your children's needs and stop seeking out specific advice from others – especially if you find (as I often did!) that it is conflicting (e.g. 'Never take a child to a minder before he or she is three because . . .'/'Always start children with a minder before they reach their second birthday because . . .').

Secondly, give yourself as much time as possible to do some preparation work with your child, such as taking some or all of the following steps:

- Start talking about the separation (whatever it is) weeks or days beforehand in a positive way.
- Refer to it as an event that has already taken place, while making a link with some other positive happening ('At Christmas when you'll have been at . . . school for three months, we will be able to . . .').
- Make a link between the event and the exciting process of growing up.
- Avoid using comparisons with other children's progress ('Johnny has already started to . . .') and stop other children from doing so if possible (e.g. 'She's a baby. When I was six, I'd been to . . .').
- Remind them of successful steps which they have already taken.
- Share any positive similar experience you may have had and refrain from bringing up your own negative memories which

could be surfacing (e.g. the nightmare tonsil operation you had at age seven). Talk about these memories to another adult if they do need an airing.

- Show your children the place they will be going to, either in reality or through pictures (e.g. the school, hospital, holiday camp, etc.).
- Arrange an introduction with an adult who will be looking after them or get a picture if possible. Alternatively, arrange for them to meet another child who has been to the place before.
- If the separation involves an overnight stay, start packing a bag of special 'goodies' well before going (e.g. pictures, a toy or a more 'grown-up' new garment, a decorated card with telephone numbers on, etc.).
- Remind your children of their relaxation games and symbols.
- Reassure them about what you will be doing, giving them a positive picture (rather than one of a parent paralysed with anxiety and longing!).
- Arrange a short trial if this is possible or appropriate (e.g. staying away for one night at first, or letting them make a bus journey on their own or having a tent in the garden).
- Talk about how excited you are at the prospect of 'hearing all about it' on their return.

Give them information and skills for independence

There is no doubt that the world is a very complex place to be in nowadays, and even the most educated and skilled among us will feel very lost and small in many situations. We have a responsibility to teach our children to accept that 'pure' independence is now virtually impossible to achieve; nevertheless, the more kitted out with survival skills and knowledge we are, the more confident we will feel and the more competent we will be out in the competitive (but exciting) jungle that society has become. So, apart from a good sound education

which will equip them with earning potential, we need to *try* to ensure that, on leaving home, our children also have, for example:

– a sound grasp of the value of money and how to manage it
– knowledge of self-defence
– knowledge of physical and emotional health care
– an understanding of household management
– relationship skills (including sexual ones)
– team skills (and when possible leadership skills)
– a good-enough understanding of how their society is administered and governed
– knowledge of their basic legal rights
– an understanding of how to obtain extra information and help when they need it

Wouldn't your emergence into early adulthood have felt a lot more secure with all the above firmly fixed in your head and your heart?!

The flight to the outside world

'Fostering independence is more loving than taking care of people who could otherwise take care of themselves.'

M. Scott Peck

Perhaps one of the reasons many parents cling to their nurturing role too long is that they have heard so many negative messages about how awful the 'letting go' process can be. We all hear many variations on the themes of 'Enjoy them while you can . . .' or 'Wait until they . . .' But the process of helping confident, positive-thinking children take their first steps into the world can be as exciting and rewarding as any other aspect of parenting. Not long ago I myself experienced one of the most powerful and memorable moments of joy of my life. It happened quite spontaneously, and quite unexpectedly, as I sat with my family in a restaurant. We were celebrating my elder daughter's 20th birthday on her return from a trip around the world, and her 16-year-old sister's return from her own independent holiday in Spain. For the previous few hours I had been totally enraptured by their stories of exciting new experiences and the challenges they courageously and skilfully survived when, suddenly, I became aware of an intense feeling of happiness and peace.

I am aware that the gift of confidence does not come with a lifetime guarantee. But, in spite of needing a recharge from time to time, it can certainly provide its owners with a seemingly endless supply of dependable emotional strength and positive potential.

Good luck with the building and boosting of this priceless present for your children – and I hope that you too will enjoy its rewards!

Further reading

Virgina Axline, *Dibs: In Search of Self* (Ballantyne, 1969)

Bruno Bettleheim, *The Good Enough Parent* (Thames and Hudson, 1987)

John Bradshaw, *Homecoming/Reclaiming and Championing Your Inner Child* (Piatkus, 1990)

Nathaniel Branden, *The Power of Self-esteem* (Health Communications, 1992)

Dorothy Briggs, *Your Child's Self-esteem: The Key to His Life* (Doubleday, 1970)

Judith Brown, *I Only Want What's Best for You* (Cedar, 1986)

Michael and Sheila Cole, *The Development of Children* (Scientific American Books, 1989)

Don Dinkmeyer and Gary D. McKay, *The Parent's Handbook* (American Guidance Service, 1989)

Adele Faber and Elaine Mazlish, *How to Talk So Kids Will Listen & Listen So Kids Will Talk* (Avon, 1980)

Susan Forward, *Toxic Parents* (Bantam, 1990)

Thomas Gordon, *P.E.T. Parent Effectiveness Training* (Plume, 1975)

Shad Helmstetter, *Predictive Parenting: What to Say When You Talk to Your Kids* (Pocket Books, 1989)

Penelope Leach, *Your Baby and Child: From Birth to Age Five* (Knopf, 1981)

David Lewis, *How to Be A Gifted Parent* (Pan, 1979)
——, *Helping Your Anxious Child* (Methuen, 1989)
Gael Lindenfield, *Assert Yourself* (Thorsons, 1986)
——, *Super Confidence* (Thorsons, 1989)
——, *The Positive Woman* (Thorsons, 1992)
——, *Managing Anger* (Thorsons, 1993)
Sarah Litvintoff, *The RELATE Guide to Better Relationships* (Ebury Press, 1991)
Joy Melville and Fiona Subotsky, *Does My Child Need Help?* (Optima, 1992)
Alice Miller, *The Drama of Being a Child* (Virago, 1986)
John Pearce, *Worries and Fears* (Thorsons, 1989)
——, *Families and Friends* (Thorsons, 1991)
——, *Bad Behaviour, Tempers and Tantrums* (Thorsons, 1993)
——, *Good Habits, Bad Habits* (Thorsons, 1994)
——, *Growth and Development* (Thorsons, 1994)
M. Scott Peck, *The Road Less Travelled* (Arrow, 1978)
Adam Phillips *Winnicott* (Fontana, 1988)
Anthony Robbins, *Awaken the Giant Within* (Simon & Schuster, 1992)
Virginia Satir, *Peoplemaking* (Souvenir Press, 1978)
Robin Skynner and John Cleese, *Families and How to Survive Them* (Methuen, 1993)
Manon Woodman, *Leaving My Father's House: Journey to Conscious Femininity* (Rider, 1993)

CASSETTES

Gael Lindenfield has made a number of personal–development cassettes which could be helpful for parents of older children. Each is designed as a self-help programme of exercises to be used on a regular basis. The list of titles includes:

- The Super Confidence Workout
- The Anger Control Workout
- The Positive Power Workout

For further information, telephone (0399) 870257 (24–hour message service)

Index

THE LAURA LINDENFIELD FOUNDATION

In 1996 Gael Lindenfield established a charity whose aim is to help teenagers and young people to establish their full potential, giving them opportunities for creativity, experience, learning and personal development.

Establishing such a foundation has long been a cherished wish of Gael's. Then, following the death of her 19 year old daughter, Laura, in a car accident on January 28th, 1996, she established the Laura Lindenfield Foundation.

The Foundation will offer both cash grants and, via its network of Friends, work placements in diverse international environments.

If you are interested in hearing more about the Laura Lindenfield Foundation, whether you wish to become a Friend, make a donation or find out how it could benefit you or a young person you know, contact Gael Lindenfield at:

11 King Alfred Place
Winchester
Hampshire
SO23 7DF

or:

Thorsons
HarperCollins*Publishers*
77–85 Fulham Palace Road
London W6 8JB

ALL ROYALTIES FROM *CONFIDENT CHILDREN* WILL BE DONATED TO THE LAURA LINDENFIELD FOUNDATION.